Acknowledgement is
made to the Dorset
County Museum, a source
of much information
for the maps & sketches.

• • •

The cover design depicts
the beautiful Rectory at
Came, William Barnes' home
at the time of his death.

EDITED WITH
FOREWORD, AFTERWORD and GLOSSARY
© ALAN CHEDZOY 1978
COVER MAPS and SKETCHES
© ERIC RICKETTS 1978

Published by **Weymouth Bookshop Ltd**
Printed by Friary Press Ltd, Dorchester
ISBN 0 905900 03 0

POEMS
GRAVE and GAY

By
WILLIAM BARNES

Weymouth Bookshop Ltd
Weymouth, Dorset
1978

Old Sturminster Newton.

· 1801 ~ 1818 ·

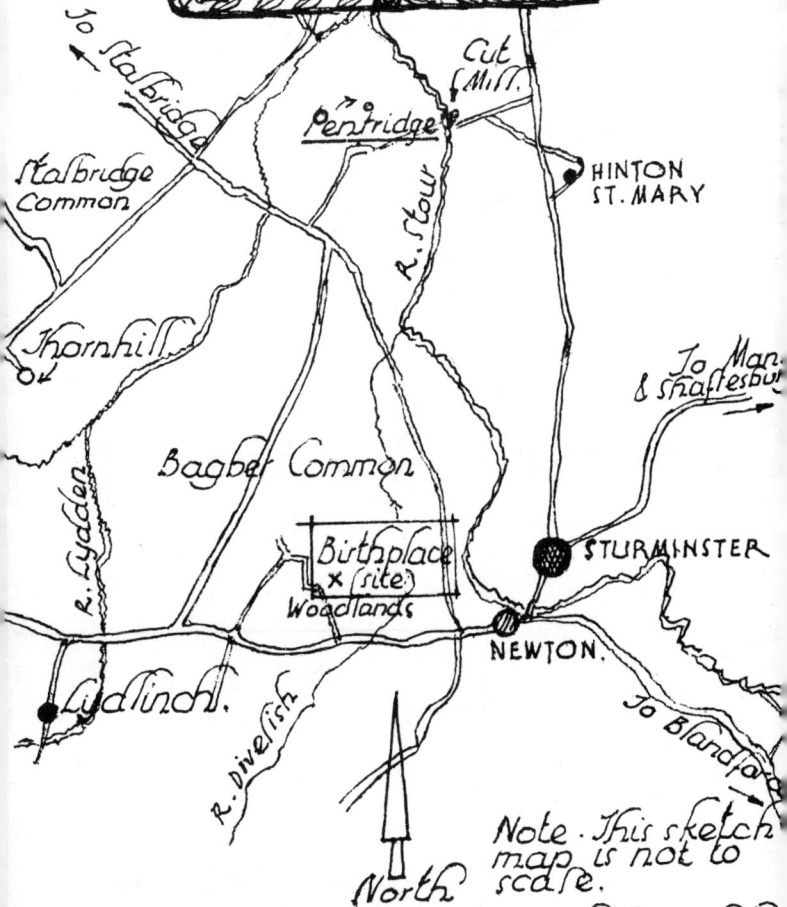

· EARLY YEARS ·
in the district of
~ STURMINSTER ~
NEWTON

To Stalbridge

Cut Mill

Pentridge

Stalbridge
Common

R. Stour

HINTON
ST. MARY

Thornhill

To Man
& Shaftesbury

Bagber Common

R. Lydden

Birthplace
× site
Woodlands

STURMINSTER

NEWTON.

Lydlinch.

R. Divelish

To Blandford

Note. This sketch
map is not to
scale.

North

The title enclosure design above is of the gold
shoe buckles worn by W.B. now in D.C. Museum

This Collection of
Poems was selected
by Giles Dugdale

originally published
June 1949.
re-printed June 1972.

NEW EDITION   1978

With a Fore Word, After Word &
Glossary by Alan Chedzoy B.A., Ph.D.

o o o

The Cover, Maps and Sketches
by Eric Ricketts.

Contents

Fore Word
The Life of William Barnes (1801–1886)

William Barnes is known today chiefly as a Dorset dialect poet, yet this reputation diminishes his actual achievement. He was a learned antiquarian and philologist. He was a prolific writer on a variety of topics and wrote, among other things, a commercial dictionary, a text-book on logic and a treatise on the hanging of gates. His two early books of poetry, *Poetical Pieces* (1820) and *Orra: a Lapland tale* (1822), were both composed in standard English, as were the *Poems of Rural Life in Common English* published in 1868. Yet it was the three volumes of 'Hwomely rhymes' written in the Dorset dialect that eventually made his name, though for many years his reputation was a small one and largely restricted to his own county of Dorset.

Barnes lived and worked all of his eighty-six years in the county save for the twelve years he spent as a schoolmaster just over the border at Mere in Wiltshire. He was born in 1801 at Bagber near Sturminster Newton in the Vale of Blackmoor. His father, John Barnes, was a small farmer from an old family that had come down in the world. Barnes always recognised that he came of humble stock. Once, when talking to a Working Men's Institute in 1857, he declared that he was not nursed in luxury but was a working man like themselves.

i

His life is best understood as a journey from obscurity to serenity and limited recognition. Like the protagonist of Hardy's *Jude the Obscure*, the life of Barnes was characterised by industry and his thought infused with a powerful intelligence. Unlike Jude, he seems not to have been troubled by religious doubt. For this reason, one refuge remained open to him when, in middle life, his boarding-school nearly failed. The role of a country clergyman offered him a limited social status and also the income and leisure to pursue his artistic and scholarly interests. Without such possibilities his life could well have ended in tragedy like that of Jude. This is not to say that he thought from the outset of the church as a calling. The biography written by his daughter, Lucy Baxter ('Leader Scott'), gives no indication of a powerful calling to the church but rather of a simple, unwavering faith that lasted a lifetime. In the course of his life he was obliged to follow whatever vocation presented itself.

The first fourteen years of his life were spent in the wooded Vale of Blackmoor and he celebrated this period in the poem 'Rustic Childhood'. He attended the Dame school in the village and later went to an 'endowed school' in Sturminster. He was a delicate and slight child and, before he was five, his mother worried about his physical incapacity for manual labour and the difficulty of his finding a fitting occupation in life. Luckily, his intellect was soon apparent. In 1814 a solicitor from Sturminster, a Mr. Dashwood, enquired at the school for a boy to copy deeds for him and Barnes was the obvious choice. After four years with Dashwood, Barnes left

Blackmoor for the first time and went to work for another solicitor, Mr. Coombs of Dorchester.

In the county town, with which his name was later to be so closely associated, he first roomed with a young man named William Carey, above a pastry-cook's shop kept by a Mr. Hazard. Here he began to develop those studies which were to prove a life-long interest. The Rector of St. Peter's, Mr. Richman, gave him tuition in the classics; Barnes taught himself wood-engraving and produced illustrations for a guidebook to Dorchester; he wrote and published two small volumes of poetry and was even referred to by a fellow-citizen as 'the Poet Laureate of Dor-chester'. Shortly after his arrival in the town he acquired another interest when he observed a sixteen-year-old girl, dressed in blue, descending from a stagecoach. It was Julia Miles, come with her father, who was an excise officer newly quartered in the town. Barnes decided at once that the girl would be his wife.

He succeeded in establishing a relationship with Julia and it developed so well that he must soon have been preoccupied with the problem of earning enough to support a wife. He thought of becoming an engraver and friends sent specimens of his work to a London firm for appraisal. They replied by praising his talents but advising further training. He could not afford such training and so, eventually, preferred to take advantage of a different opportunity that presented itself. William Carey reported that the master of his old school at Mere, in Wiltshire, was leaving his post, and Carey was happy to recommend Barnes as a successor. Julia encouraged him to apply for the post despite the separation it would bring them. She declared that she would take pupils herself so that later she might be a help to him. He decided to accept the post and thus his first profession was chosen. He was to become a schoolmaster.

For four years in Mere he lived a lonely life in lodgings, one of teaching, saving and study. His self-cultivation was amazingly industrious. An old French surgeon, M. Masson, gave him French conversation. Barnes began to read in Latin, Greek, Persian, Russian, German and Italian, and, from time to time, kept a diary in the two latter languages. He practised drawing and employed his wood engraving to provide illustrations for a new book on Somerset.

After four years of bachelor life he felt that at last he was able to be married. Julia and he took Chantry House, in Mere, and supplemented their income by taking in boarders. The house had belonged to the Grove family who were friends of Charles II. Barnes and Julia loved the garden especially. When they left Chantry House in 1835 he wrote the poignant poem 'To a Garden—On Leaving It' in which he recollects how he loved to scythe the grass in the early morning.

At Chantry House his private studies seemed only to increase. His reading was immense. A record of his reading in 1830 includes German and Russian texts, logic, Welsh, Greek and even Hindustani, a language important to those of his scholars seeking to gain entrance to the Indian Civil Service by means of public examination. Barnes began those studies in poetic structure in Italian, Welsh and Persian which he was later to employ in the composition of poems in English. He wrote sonnets in English and Italian.

iv

Yet his interests were never restricted to scholarship. He was concerned with social questions and published pieces in the *Dorset County Chronicle* above the name 'Dilettante'. He loved carving, carpentering, gardening, turning his own chessmen, playing the flute, piano and violin, visiting the church to play the organ, play-going (he once went to the travelling players every night for a week), writing poems and a farce, inventing and trying out swimming shoes (they did not work), developing his knowledge of archaeology and also of mathematics with the help of his friend, General Shrapnel. Save for Julia, he was largely isolated intellectually, yet the list of his interests vividly witnesses the need of a powerful creative intelligence to seize upon every occupation which offers it scope for employment.

While at Mere he published the first of his books on philological subjects, *An Etymological Glossary* (1829). In all he published thirty-four books or pamphlets beside a great many uncollected essays and poems in newspapers and journals such as *Macmillan's Magazine*. Many of his articles and books are philological in subject matter and it is significant that Lucy Baxter describes her father, in the title of her book, as 'Poet and Philologist'. Poetry and Philology were closely related for him. Lucy Baxter notes that her father first began to write his dialect poems in the 'hope of preserving, and dream of restoring this pure ancient language'.

In 1835 Barnes and his family left Mere, and the Blackmoor Vale, for good. He removed his school to Dorchester where he was to teach for twenty-seven years, at first in Durngate Street and subsequently in South Street. In these early years of his Dorchester school, readers of the *Dorset County Chronicle* first became familiar with the anonymous dialect poems that appeared fairly regularly in a certain corner of the paper. Their authorship became known in 1844 when he brought out *Poems of rural Life in the Dorset dialect, with a dissertation and glossary*, which was to be reprinted three times. The poems in the press attracted a good deal of correspondence and were seen primarily as social comment. The Hon. Mrs. Caroline Norton was one of Barnes's first admirers and strove to bring him to the attention of more cultivated and influential people. In 1844, Barnes was invited to Frampton House, where his simple dignity gained him much respect among the fashionable guests of Mr. Richard Brinsley Sheridan. Mrs. Norton arranged a London reading of his poems for him, before a very distinguished audience. Unfortunately, this had to be postponed for a considerable time. The Dorset poems seemed to have achieved satisfactory sales in London reckoned by what could be expected of work not expressed in standard English.

Yet Barnes did not prosper. His scholarship and poetry brought in very little. Despite the friendship of such men as Coventry Patmore and Francis Turner Palgrave, he remained a little-known, provincial figure. Locally, he did begin to acquire a kind of recognition. He and the Rev. C. W. Bingham became the first secretaries to the new Dorset County Museum, founded by those who were alarmed that the richness of Dorset's antiquities might be severely damaged by the cuttings and tunnels constructed as extensions to the London-Dorchester Railway in 1845. Yet, despite his prestige as a local poet and antiquarian, he was passed over in the choice for the head-mastership of Hardye's Grammar School in Dorchester. He was well supported by testimonials from the local M.P. and other county dignatories but the 'feoffees', or governors, denied him the election by restricting the choice to one in holy orders. Perhaps he struck them as an alarmingly-eccentric candidate, neither a grammar-school man nor a graduate; one who wrote poems in common speech forms and wore an antiquated cloak in the street. He was subsequently rejected in his application for the headship of Bath Grammar School and even for the chaplaincy of the local asylum.

The most grievous blow of all, in these years of disappointment, was the death of his wife, Julia, in 1852. He felt her loss for the rest of his life and frequently concluded a day's entry in his Italian diary with the word, 'Giulia', written, as his daughter remarked, like a sigh. His loss prompted, over the years, some of his most beautiful and poignant poems including 'The Wife A-Lost' and 'Woak Hill' printed here.

His refuge was the church. From 1847–1852 he had been the curate of the little church of Whitcombe, walking from Dorchester each Sunday to minister to the small congregation. He gave up the 'donative' of Whitcombe, worth thirteen guineas a year, at the time of his wife's illness. After her death, applications to his school unaccountably diminished and he must have thought more and more of entering the church as an answer to his problems. He had registered as a 'ten year' man at St. John's College, Cambridge, and in 1850, he was awarded the degree of B.D. He had already been ordained in 1848. His financial problems were only partly solved by the granting of a Civil List pension of £70, in 1861. Greater help came in 1862 when Colonel Damer was enabled to fulfil his promise to Barnes of the living of Winterbourne Came, which included the curacy of Whitcombe.

The last twenty-four years of his life were spent in the old Rectory at Winterbourne Came, a thatched house on the road to Dorchester that acted as home for the poet, his son, four daughters and grand-children. By this time he had become a figure cel-ebrated far beyond the county borders, the friend of Edmund Gosse, Tennyson and Palgrave. The young Thomas Hardy noted with humour and affection the appearance of the aged poet striding into Dorchester on market day clad in 'caped cloak, knee breeches and buckled shoes with a leather satchel'. This costume, Barnes claimed, was proof against all weathers and he ignored the elements while making the long walks about his parish until he was well over eighty. A photograph of him in his eighties reveals a venerable figure, with white flowing beard, with children and grandchildren in the garden at Came. He had become revered and respected, a sage and polymath, living out his life in a paradise lapped still by the sea of faith. He is buried in the churchyard at Winterbourne Came and his grave is marked with a Celtic cross.

In February 1887, the Bishop of Salisbury unveiled a statue of Barnes outside St. Peter's in Dorchester. The bronze plate is inscribed with a passage from a dialect poem that Barnes most probably read in many a Working Men's Institute and which his listeners could now apply, in memory, to the poet. It is from 'Culver Dell':

> 'But now I hope his kindly feace
> Is gone to find a better pleace;
> But still, wi vo'k a-left behind
> He'll always be a-kept in mind.'

Alan Chedzoy,
Weymouth,
February, 1978

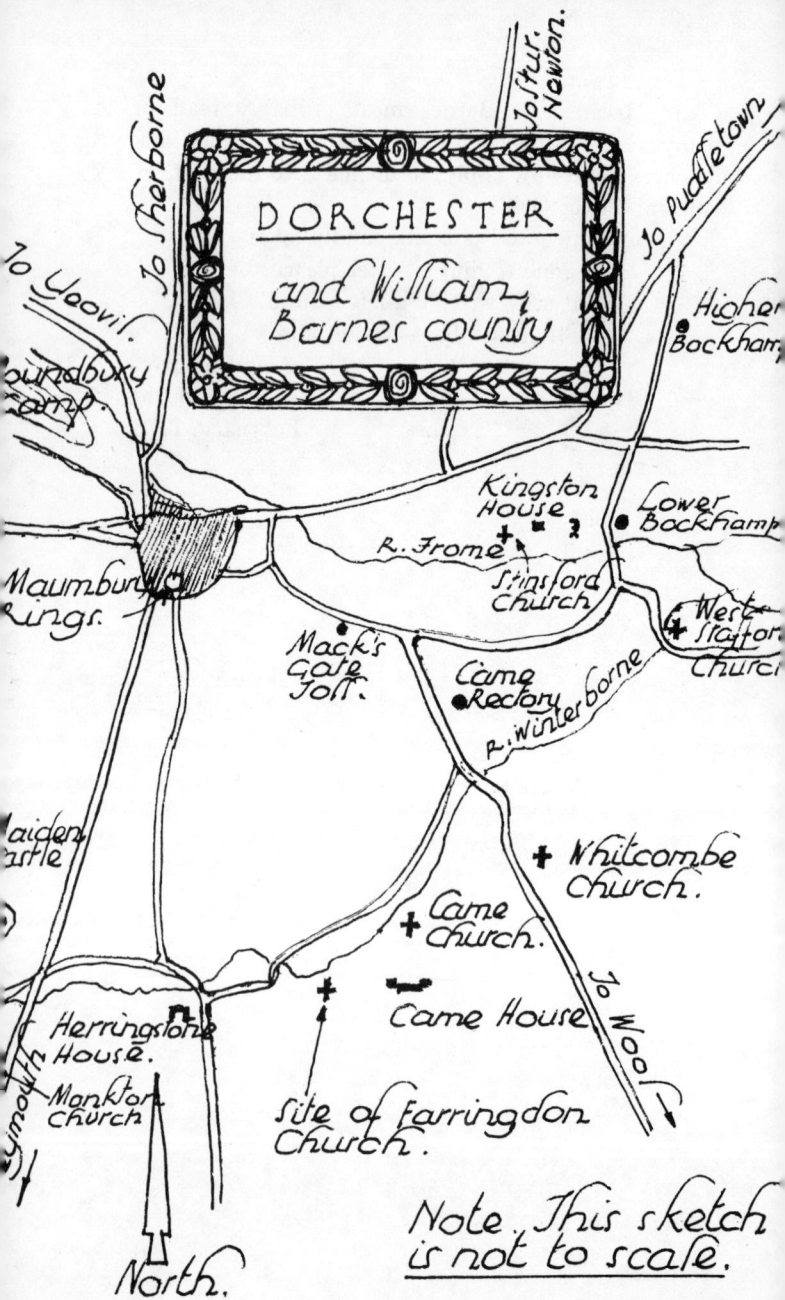

DORCHESTER

and William Barnes country

To Sturi. Newton.

To Puddletown

To Sherborne

To Yeovil.

Poundbury Camp.

Higher Bockham.

Kingston House

R. Frome

Lower Bockhamp.

Maumbury Rings.

Stinsford Church.

Wert Stafford Church.

Mack's Gate Toll.

Came Rectory

R. Winterborne

Maiden Castle

Whitcombe Church.

Came Church.

To Wool.

Weymouth

Herringstone House.

Came House

Monkton Church

site of Farringdon Church.

North.

Note. This sketch is not to scale.

PRAISE O' DO'SET

We Do'set, though we mid be hwomely,
   Be'nt asheam'd to own our pleace ;
An' we've zome women not uncomely ;
   Nor asheam'd to show their feace :
We've a mead or two wo'th mowen,
We've an ox or two wo'th showen,
     In the village,
     At the tillage,
Come along an' you shall vind
That Do'set men don't sheame their kind.
     Friend an' wife,
     Fathers, mothers, sisters, brothers,
     Happy, happy, be their life !
     Vor Do'set dear,
     Then gi'e woone cheer ;
     D'ye hear ? woone cheer !

If you in Do'set be a-roamen,
   An' ha' business at a farm,
Then woon't ye zee your eale a-foamen !
   Or your cider down to warm ?
Woon't ye have brown bread a-put ye,
An' some vinny cheese a-cut ye ?
     Butter ?—rolls o't !
     Cream ?—why bowls o't !
Woon't ye have, in short, your vill,
A-gi'ed wi' a right good will ?

Friend an' wife,
Fathers, mothers, sisters, brothers,
Happy, happy, be their life !
Vor Do'set dear,
Then gi'e woone cheer :
D'ye hear ? woone cheer ;

An' woon't ye have vor ev'ry shillen,
    Shillen's wo'th at any shop,
Though Do'set chaps be up to zellen,
    An' can meake a tidy swop ?
Use 'em well, they'll use you better ;
In good turns they woon't be debtor.
        An' so comely,
        An' so hwomely,
Be the maidens, if your son
Took woone o'm, then you'd cry " Well
    done ! "
        Friend an' wife,
        Fathers, mothers, sisters, brothers,
        Happy, happy, be their life !
        Vor Do'set dear,
        Then gi'e woone cheer ;
        D'ye hear ? woone cheer !

If you do zee our good men travel,
    Down a-voot, or on their meares,
Along the winden leanes o' gravel,
    To the markets or the feairs,—
Though their ho'ses cwoats be ragged,
Though the men be muddy-lagged,
        Be they roughish,
        Be they gruffish,

2

They be sound, an' they will stand
By what is right wi' heart an' hand.
 Friend an' wife,
 Fathers, mothers, sisters, brothers,
 Happy, happy, be their life !
 Vor Do'set dear,
 Then gi'e woone cheer ;
 D'ye hear ? woone cheer !

RUSTIC CHILDHOOD

No city primness train'd my feet
To strut in childhood through the street,
But freedom let them loose to tread
The yellow cowslips' downcast head ;
Or climb, above the twining hop
And ivy, to the elm-tree's top ;
Where southern airs of blue-sky'd day
Breath'd o'er the daisy and the may.
    I knew you young, and love you now,
    O shining grass, and shady bough.

Far off from town, where splendour tries
To draw the looks of gather'd eyes,
And clocks, unheeded, fail to warn
The loud-tongued party of the morn,
I spent in woodland shades my day
In cheerful work or happy play.
And slept at night where rustling leaves
Threw moonlight shadows o'er my eaves.
    I knew you young, and love you now,
    O shining grass, and shady bough.

Or in the grassy drove by ranks
Of white-stemm'd ashes, or by banks
Of narrow lanes, in-winding round
The hedgy sides of shelving ground ;

4

Where low-shot light struck in to end
Again at some cool-shaded bend,
Where we might see through dark leav'd boughs
The evening light on green hill-brows.
  I knew you young, and love you now,
  O shining grass, and shady bough.

Or on the hillock where I lay
At rest on some bright holyday ;
When short noon-shadows lay below
The thorn in blossom white as snow ;
And warm air bent the glist'ning tops
Of bushes in the lowland copse,
Before the blue hills swelling high
And far against the southern sky.
  I knew you young, and love you now,
  O shining grass, and shady bough.

WHITE AND BLUE

My love is of comely height and straight,
And comely in all her ways and gait,
She shows in her face the rose's hue,
And her lids on her eyes, are white on blue.

When Elemley club-men walk'd in May,
And folk came in clusters every way,
As soon as the sun dried up the dew,
And clouds in the sky were white on blue,

She came by the down with tripping walk,
By daisies and shining banks of chalk,
And brooks with the crowfoot flow'rs to strew
The sky-tinted water, white on blue ;

She nodded her head as play'd the band,
She tapp'd with her foot as she did stand,
She danc'd in a reel, and wore all new
A skirt with a jacket, white and blue.

I singled her out from thin and stout,
From slender and stout I chose her out,
And what in the evening could I do
But give her my breast-knot white and blue ?

LINES ADDRESSED TO AN OAK NEAR MY FATHER'S COTTAGE

(One of William Barnes's earliest printed poems.)

Yes, lonely tree, th' autumnal gust assails
    Thy naked limbs, that tremble as it blows ;
Ah ! soon, full soon, expos'd to colder gales,
    Those limbs may bend beneath December snows

Oft have I sat in thy expansive head,
    A fancied monarch of the space below ;
Oft on thy trunk my youthful cheek I've laid,
    Wet with the tears I shed for fancied woe.

Subdued by time, full many a branch decays,
    That green and flourishing thou borest then ;
Subdued by time, the passions of those days
    Will never bloom within my breast again.

No more, persisting through the tangled briar,
    To pluck the primrose from yon bank I try ;
No more I feel the puerile desire
    To seize each bird that whistling flutters by.

The objects that in infancy we crave,
    Cease to delight us as we grow in years ;
Th' expanding mind, as we approach the grave,
    To trivial youthful joys no more adheres.

Till ling'ring joyless, impotent, and old,
  The man around him casts his torpid eyes ;
And cold to life, to all its pleasures cold,
  Just heaves his aged breast, and calmly dies.

THE BROKEN JUG

JENNY AND TOM

(Tom idly swings about Jenny's jug, and breaks it against a stone.)

J. As if you could not leave the jug alone !
   Now you have smack'd my jug ;
   Now you have whack'd my jug ;
   Now you have crack'd my jug,

   Against the stone.

T. The jug was crack'd before, unknown to you :
   So don't belie the stone ;
   It scarce went nigh the stone,
   It just went by the stone,

   And broke in two.

J. Oh ! crack'd before ! no ! that was sound enough,
   From back to lip was sound,
   To stand or tip was sound,
   To hold or dip, was sound.

   Don't talk such stuff.

T. How high then must I take its price to reach ?
   I'd buy some more as good ;
   I'd buy a score as good ;
   I'd buy a store as good ;

   For twopence each.

9

D

J. Indeed ! when stonen jugs are sold so dear !
    No, there's a tap for lies ;
    And there's a slap for lies ;
    And there's a rap for lies,

                                    About your ear.

T. Oh ! there are pretty hands ! a little dear !

PLORATA VERIS LACHRYMIS

My Julia, my dearest bride,
Since thou hast left my lonely side,
My life has lost its hope and zest.
The sun rolls on from east to west,
But brings no more that evening rest,
Thy loving kindness made so sweet,
And time is slow that once was fleet,
  As day by day was waning.

The last sad day that show'd thee lain
Before me, smiling in thy pain,
The sun soar'd high along his way
To mark the longest summer day,
And show to me the latest play
Of thy sweet smile, and thence, as all
The days' lengths shrunk from small to small,
  My joy began its waning.

And now 'tis keenest pain to see
Whate'er I saw in bliss with thee.
The softest airs that ever blow,
The fairest days that ever glow,
Unfelt by thee, but bring me woe ;
And sorrowful I kneel in pray'r,
Which thou no longer, now, canst share,
  As day by day is waning.

11

How can I live my lonesome days ?
How can I tread my lonesome ways ?
How can I take my lonesome meal ?
Or how outlive the grief I feel ?
Or how again look on to weal ?
Or sit, at rest, before the heat
Of winter fires, to miss thy feet,
     When evening light is waning.

Thy voice is still I loved to hear,
Thy voice is lost I held so dear.
Since death unlocks thy hand from mine,
No love awaits me such as thine ;
Oh ! boon the hardest to resign !
But if we meet again at last
In heav'n I little care how fast
     My life may now be waning.

TOKENS

Green mwold on zummer bars do show
   That they've a-dripp'd in winter wet ;
The hoof-worn ring o' groun' below
   The tree, do tell o' storms or het ;
The trees in rank along a ledge
Do show where woonce did bloom a hedge ;
An' where the vurrow-marks do stripe
The down, the wheat woonce rustled ripe.
Each mark ov things a-gone vrom view—
To eyezight's woone, to soulzight two.

The grass agean the mwoldren door
   'S a token sad o' vo'k a-gone,
An' where the house, bwoth wall an' vloor,
   'S a-lost, the well mid linger on.
What tokens, then, could Meary gi'e
That she's a-liv'd, an' liv'd vor me,
But things a-done vor thought an' view ?
Good things that nwone agean can do,
An' every work her love ha' wrought
To eyezight's woone, but two to thought.

13

FARMER'S SONS

Ov all the chaps a-burnt so brown
   By zunny hills an' hollors,
Or all the whindlen chaps in town
   Wi' backs so weak as rollers,
There's narn that's half so light o' heart,
   (I'll bet, if thou't zay " done," min,)
An' narn that's half so strong an' smart,
   'S a merry farmer's son, min.

He'll fling a stwone so true's a shot,
   He'll jump so light's a cat ;
He'll heave a waight up that would squot
   A weakly fellow flat.
He wont gi'e up when things don't fay,
   But turn em into fun, min ;
An' what's hard work to zome, is play
   Avore a farmer's son, min.

His bwony earm an' knuckly vist
   ('Tis best to meake a friend o't)
Would het a fellow, that's a-miss'd,
   Half backward wi' the wind o't.
Wi' such a chap at hand, a maid
   Would never goo a nun, min ;
She'd have noo call to be afraid
   Bezide a farmer's son, min.

He'll turn a vurrow, drough his langth,
   So straight as eyes can look,
Or pitch all day, wi' half his strangth,
   At ev'ry pitch a pook ;
An' then goo vower mile, or vive,
   To vind his friends in fun, min,
Vor maiden's be but dead alive
   'I thout a farmer's son, min.

Zoo jay be in his heart so light,
   An' manly feace so brown ;
An' health goo wi' en hwome at night,
   Vrom mead, or wood, or down.
O' rich an' poor, o' high an' low,
   When all's a-said an' done, min,
The smartest chap that I do know,
   'S a worken farmer's son, min.

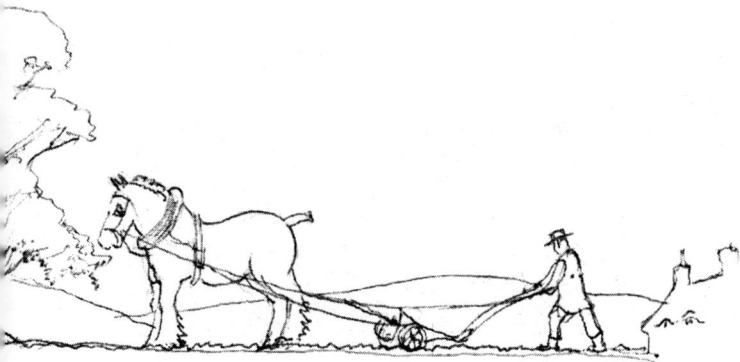

SONNET

LEAVES

Leaves of the summer, lovely summer's pride,
  Sweet is the shade below your silent tree,
Whether in waving copses, where ye hide
  My roamings, or in fields that let me see
  The open sky ; and whether ye may be
Around the low-stemm'd oak, robust and wide ;
Or taper ash upon the mountain side ;
  Or lowland elm ; your shade is sweet to me.

Whether ye wave above the early flow'rs
  I' lively green ; or whether, rustling sere,
  Ye fly on playful winds, around my feet,

In dying autumn ; lovely are your bow'rs,
  Ye early-dying children of the year ;
  Holy the silence of your calm retreat.

THE WOODLAND HOME

My woodland home, where hillocks swell
With flow'ry sides, above the dell,
And sedge's hanging ribbons gleam
By meadow withies in the stream ;
And elms, with ground-beglooming shades,
Stand high upon the sloping glades.
When toilsome day at evening fades,
    And trials agitate my breast,
      By fancy brought,
      I come in thought
To thee my home, my spirit's rest.

I left thy woody fields that lay
So fair below my boyhood's play,
To toil in busy life that fills
The world with strife of wayward wills ;
Where mortals in their little day
Of pride disown their brother clay.
But when my soul can steal away
    From such turmoil, with greater zest
      By fancy brought
      I come in thought
To thee my home, my spirit's rest.

For I behold thee fresh and fair
In summer light, and summer air,

17

As when I rambled, pulling low
The hazel bough that, when let go,
Flew back, with high-toss'd head, upright,
To rock again in airy light,
Where brown-stemm'd elms and ashes white
   Rose tall upon the flow'ry breast
     Of some green mound,
     With timber crown'd,
My woodland home, my spirit's rest.

And there my fancy will not find
The loveless heart or selfish mind,
Nor scowling hatred mutt'ring aught
To break my heart-intrancing thought ;
But manly souls above deceit,
And lively girls with smiles to greet
The bright'ning eyes they love to meet.
   The fairest in their looks, and best
     In heart : I found,
     On thy lov'd ground,
My woodland home, my spirit's rest.

SONNET

To a Garden—On Leaving It

Sweet garden ! peaceful spot ! no more in thee
    Shall I e'er while away the sunny hour.
Farewell each blooming shrub, and lofty tree ;
    Farewell the mossy path and nodding flow'r :
    I shall not hear again from yonder bow'r
The song of birds, or humming of the bee,
Nor listen to the waterfall, nor see
    The clouds float on behind the lofty tow'r.

No more, at breezy eve, or dewy morn,
    My gliding scythe shall shear thy mossy green :
My busy hands shall never more adorn,

    My eyes no more may see, this peaceful scene.
But still, sweet spot, wherever I may be,
My love-led soul will wander back to thee.

THE LOVE-CHILD

Where the bridge out at Woodley did stride,
  Wi' his wide arches' cool-sheaded bow,
Up above the clear brook that did slide
  By the popples, befoam'd white as snow ;
As the gil'cups did quiver among
  The white deasies, a-spread in a sheet,
There a quick-trippen maid come along,—
  Aye, a girl wi' her light-steppen veet.

An' she cried ' I do pray, is the road
  ' Out to Lincham on here, by the mead ?
An' 'oh ! yes,' I meade answer, an' show'd
  Her the way it would turn an' would lead.
' Goo alone by the beech in the nook,
  Where the children do play in the cool,
  To the steppen-stwones over the brook,—
  Aye, the grey blocks o' rock at the pool.'

' Then you don't seem a-born an' a-bred '
  I spoke up, 'at a pleace here about ' ;
An' she answer'd, wi' cheaks up as red
  As a piny but leate a-come out,
' No, I liv'd wi' my uncle that died
  Back in Eapril, an' now I'm a-come
Here to Ham, to my mother, to bide,—
  Aye, to her house to vind a new hwome.'

I'm asheam'd that I wanted to know
    Any mwore of her childhood or life,
But then, why should so feair a child grow
    Where noo father did bide wi' his wife ;
Then wi' blushes o' zunrisen morn,
    She replied, ' that it midden be known,
Oh ! they zent me away to be born,—
    Aye, they hid me when zome would be shown.'

Oh ! it meade me a'most teary-ey'd,
    An' I vound I a'most could ha' groan'd—
What ! so winnen, an' still cast a-zide—
    What ! so lovely, an' not to be own'd ;
Oh ! a God-gift a treated wi' scorn,
    Oh ! a child that a Squier should own ;
An' to zend her away to be born ! —
    Aye, to hide her where others be shown !

EVENEN' IN THE VILLAGE

Now the light o' the west is a-turn'd to gloom,
   An' the men be at hwome vrom ground ;
An' the bells be a-zenden all down the Coombe
   From tower their mwoansome sound.
      An' the wind is still,
       An' the house-dogs do bark,
An' the rooks be a-vled to the elems high an' dark,
   An' the water do roar at mill.

An' the flickeren light drough the window-peane
   Vrom the candle's dull fleame do shoot,
An' young Jemmy the smith is a-gone down leane
   A-playen his shrill-vaiced flute.
      An' the miller's man
       Do zit down at his ease
On the seat that is under the cluster o' trees,
   Wi' his pipe an' his cider can.

SAM'EL DOWN VROM LON'ON

When Cousin Sam come down vrom Lon'on,
Along at vu'st I wer' so mad wi'n,
He though hizzelf so very cunnen ;
But eet, vor all, what fun we had wi'n !
Why, if a goose did only wag her tail,
An' come a-hissen at his lags, she'd zet en
A-meaken off behine a wall or rail
A-waken, but as vast as shame would let en.
Or if a zow did nod her lop-ear'd head,
A-trotten an' a-grunten wi' her litter,
She'd put the little chap in zich a twitter,
His vaice did quiver in his droat wi' dread,
An' if a bull did screape the ground an' bleare,
His dizzy head did poke up every heair.
An' eet he thought hizzelf a goodish rider,
An' we all thought there werden many woo'se ;
'E zot upon the meare so scram's a spider,
A-holden on the web o'n, when 'tis loose.
Oone day, when we wer' all a little idle,
He zaid he'd have a ride upon the hoss a bit.
An' Sorrell when she vound en pull the bridle
In his queer way, begun to prance an' toss a bit.
An' he did knit his brows, an' scwold the meare,
An' she agean did trample back an' rear,
A-woonderen who 'twer' she had to zit zoo,
An' what queer han' di tuggy at her bit zoo.

23

But when she got her head a little rightish,
She carr'd en off, while we did nearly split
Our zides a-laefen, vor to zee en zit,
If zit he did, an' that did meake en spitish.
Zoo on 'e rod so fine, a poken out
His two splay veet avore en, all astrout,
A-flappen up his elbows, lik' two wings,
To match the hosses steps, wi' timely springs.
But there, poor Sam'el hadded gone
Droo Hwomegroun' when wold Sorrel shied
At zome 'hat there, an' sprung azide
An' shot off Sam'el lik' a bag o' bron.
'E vell, 'tis true, upon a grassy hump,
But nearly squilch'd his breath out wi' the thump,
An' squot the sheenen hat 'e wore,
An' laid wi' all his lim's a-spread,
An' seemely so loose an' dead,
'S a doll a-cast upon a vloor.
When Cousin Sam come down vrom Lon'on,
He thought hizzelf so very cunnen.

THE SPRING

When wintry weather's all a-done,
An' brooks do sparkle in the zun,
An' naisy-builden rooks do vlee
Wi' sticks toward their elem tree ;
When birds do zing, an' we can zee
   Upon the boughs the buds o' spring,—
   Then I'm as happy as a king,
      A-vield wi' health an' zunsheen.

Vor then the cowslip's hangen flow'r
A-wetted in the zunny show'r,
Do grow wi' vi'lets, sweet o' smell,
Bezide the wood-screen'd grægle's bell ;
Where drushes' aggs, wi' sky-blue shell,
   Do lie in mossy nests among
   The thorns, while they do zing their zong
      At evenen in the zunsheen.

25

E

LEARNING

Heavenly source of guiltless joy !
  Holy friend through good and ill ;
When all idle pleasures cloy,
  Thou cans't hold my spirit still.

Take me to some still abode,
  Underneath some woody hill ;
By some timber-skirted road,
  By some willow-shaded rill.

Where along the rocky brook,
  Flying echoes sweetly sound,
And the hoarsely-croacking rook
  Builds upon the trees around.

Take me to some lofty room
  Lighted from the western sky,
Where no glare dispels the gloom
  Till the golden eve is nigh,

Where the works of searching thought,
  Chosen books, may still impart,
What the wise of old have taught,
  What has tried the meek of heart.

Books in long-dead tongues, that stirr'd
　　Living hearts in other climes ;
Telling to my eyes, unheard,
　　Glorious deeds of olden times.

Books that purify the thought,
　　Spirits of the learned dead,
Teachers of the little taught,
　　Comforters when friends are fled.

Learning ! source of guiltless joy !
　　Holy friend through good and ill,
When all idle pleasures cloy,
　　Thou cans't hold my spirit still.

THE CHILD AN' THE MOWERS

O, aye ! they had woone chile bezide,
  An' a finer your eyes never met,
'Twer a dear little fellow that died
  In the zummer that come wi' such het ;
By the mowers, too thoughtless in fun,
  He wer then a-zent off vrom our eyes,
Vrom the light ov the dew-dryen zun,—
  Aye ! vrom days under blue-hollow'd skies.

He went out to the mowers in mead,
  When the zun wer a-rwose to his height,
An' the men wer a-swingen the snead,
  Wi' their earms in white sleeves, left an' right ;
An' out there, as they rested at noon,
  O ! they drench'd en wi' eale-horns too deep,
Till his thoughts wer a-drown'd in a swoon :
  Aye ! his life wer a-smother'd in sleep.

Then they laid en there-right on the ground,
  On a grass-heap, a zweltren wi' het,
Wi' his heair all a-wetted around
  His young feace, wi' the big drops o' zweat ;
In his little left palm he'd a-zet,
  Wi' his right hand, his vore-vingers' tip,
As for zome'hat he woulden vorget,—
  Aye ! zome thought that he woulden let slip.

Then they took en in hwome to his bed,
  An' he rwose vrom his pillow noo mwore
Vor the curls on his sleek little head
  To be blown by the wind out o' door.
Vor he died while the hay russled grey
  On the staddle so leately begun :
Lik' the mown-grass a-dried by the day,—
  Aye ! the zwath-flow'r's a-kill'd by the zun.

29

GRAMMER'S SHOES

I do seem to zee Grammer as she did use
Vor to show us, at Chris'mas, her wedden shoes,
An' her flat spreaden bonnet so big an' roun'
As a girt pewter dish a-turn'd upside down ;
    When we all did draw near
    In a cluster to hear
O' the merry wold soul how she did use
To walk an' to dance wi' her high-heel shoes.

She'd a gown wi' girt flowers lik' hollyhocks,
An' zome stockens o' gramfer's a-knit wi' clocks,
An' a token she kept under lock an' key,—
A small lock ov his heair off avore't wer grey.
    An' her eyes wer red,
    An' she shook her head
When we'd all a-look'd at it, an' she did use
To lock it away wi' her wedden shoes.

She could tell us such teales about heavy snows,
An' o' rains an' o' floods when the waters rose
All up into the housen, an' carr'd awoy
All the bridge wi' a man an' his little bwoy ;
    An' o' vog an' vrost,
    An' o' v'k a-lost,
An' o' pearties at Chris'mas, when she did use
Vor to walk hwome wi' gramfer in high-heel shoes.

Evr'y Chris'mas she lik'd vor the bells to ring,
An' to have in the zingers to hear em zing
The wold carols she heard many years a-gone,
While she warm'd em zome cider avore the bron';
    An' she'd look an' smile
    At our dancen, while
She did tell how her friends now a-gone did use
To reely wi' her in their high-heel shoes.

Ah! an' how she did like vor to deck wi' red
Holly-berries the window an' wold clock's head,
An' the clavy wi' boughs o' some bright green leaves,
An' to meake twoast an' eale upon Chris'mas eves;
    But she's now, drough greace,
    In a better pleace,
Though we'll never vorget her, poor soul, nor lose
Gramfer's token ov heair, nor her wedden shoes.

FALSE FRIENDS-LIKE

When I wer still a bwoy, an' mother's pride,
A bigger bwoy spoke up to me so kind-like,
' If you do like, I'll treat ye wi' a ride
In thease wheel-barrow here.' Zoo I wer blind-like
To what he had a-worken in his mind-like,
An' mounted vor a passenger inside ;
An' comen to a puddle, perty wide,
He tipp'd me in, a-grinnen back behind-like.
Zoo when a man do come to me so thick-like,
An' sheake my hand, where woonce he pass'd me by,
An' tell me he would do me this or that,
I can't help thinken o' the big bwoy's trick-like.
An' then, vor all I can but wag my hat
An' thank en, I do veel a little shy.

OUR BE'THPLACE

How dear's the door a latch do shut,
An' gearden that a hatch do shut,
Where vu'st our bloomen cheaks ha' prest
The pillor ov our childhood's rest ;
Or where, wi' little tooes, we wore
The paths our fathers trod avore ;
Or clim'd the timber's bark aloft,
Below the zingen lark aloft,
The while we heard the echo sound
Drough all the ringen valley round.

A lwonesome grove o' woak did rise
To screen our house, where smoke did rise
A-twisten blue, while yeet the zun
Did langthen on our childhood's fun ;
An' there, wi' all the sheapes an' sounds
O' life, among the timber'd grounds,
The birds upon their boughs did zing,
An' milkmaids by their cows did zing,
Wi' merry sounds that softly died
A-ringen down the valley zide.

By river banks wi' reeds a-bound,
An' sheenen pools wi' weeds a-bound,
The long-neck'd gander's ruddy bill
To snow-white geese did cackle sh'ill ;

An' striden peewits heasten'd by,
O' tiptoe wi' their screamen cry ;
An' stalken cows a-lowen loud,
An' strutten cocks a-crowen loud,
Did rouse the echoes up to mock
Their mingled sounds by hill an' rock.

The stars that clim'd our skies all dark,
Above our sleepen eyes all dark,
An' zuns a-rollen round to bring
The seasons on vrom spring to spring,
Ha' vled, wi' never-resten flight,
Drough green-bough'd day, an' dark-tree'd night ;
Till now our childhood's pleaces there
Be gay wi' other feaces there,
An' we ourselves do vollow on
Our own vorelivers dead an' gone.

WHAT DICK AN' I DID

Last week the Browns ax'd nearly all
   The naighbours to a randy,
An' left us out, o't, gr't an' small,
   Vor all we liv'd so handy ;
An' zoo I zaid to Dick, ' We'll trudge,
   When they be in their fun, min ;
An' car up zome'hat to the rudge,
   An' jis' stop up the tun, min.'

Zoo, wi' the ladder vrom the rick,
   We stole towards the house,
An' crope in roun' behind en, lik'
   A cat upon a mouse.
Then looken roun', Dick whisper'd ' How
   Is thease job to be done, min :
Why we do want a faggot now,
   Vor stoppen up the tun, min.'

' Stan' still,' I answer'd ; ' I'll teake ceare
   O' that : why dussun zee
The little grinden-stwone out there,
   Below the apple-tree ?
Put up the ladder ; in a crack
   Shalt zee that I wull run, min,
An' teake en up upon my back,
   An' soon stop up the tun, min.'

35

Zoo up I clomb upon the thatch,
　　An clapp'd en on ; an' slided
Right down agean, an' ran drough hatch,
　　Behind the hedge, an' hided.
The vier that wer clear avore,
　　Begun to spweil their fun, min ;
The smoke all roll'd toward the door,
　　For I'd a stopp'd the tun, min.

The maidens cough'd or stopp'd their breath,
　　The men did hauk an' spet ;
The wold vo'k bundled out from he'th
　　Wi' eyes a runnen wet.
' T'ool choke us all,' the wold man cried,
　　' Whatever's to be done, min ?
Why zome'hat is a-vell inside
　　O' chimney drough the tun, min.'

Then out they scamper'd all, vull run,
　　An' out cried Tom, ' I think
The grinden-stwone is up on tun,
　　Vor I can zee the wink.
This is some kindness that the vo'k
　　At Woodley have a-done, min ;
I wish I had em here, I'd poke
　　Their numskulls down the tun, min.'

Then off he zet, an' come so quick
　　'S a lamplighter, an' brote
The little ladder in vrom rick,
　　To clear the chimney's droat.
While I, a-chucklen at the joke,
　　A-slided down to run, min,
To hide lock, had a left the vo'k
　　As bad as na'r a tun, min.

TREES BE COMPANY

When zummer's burnen het's a-shed
Upon the droopen grasses head,
A-dreven under sheady leaves
The workvo'k in their snow-white sleeves,
We then mid yearn to clim' the height,
    Where thorns be white, above the vern ;
An' air do turn the zunsheen's might
    To softer light too weak to burn—
        On woodless downs we mid be free,
        But lowland trees be company.

Though downs mid show a wider view
O' green a-reachen into blue
Than roads a-winden in the glen,
An' ringen wi' the sounds o' men ;
The thissle's crown o' red an' blue
    In Fall's cwold dew do wither brown,
An' larks come down 'ithin the lew,
    As storms do brew, an' skies do frown—
        An' though the down do let us free,
        The lowland trees be company.

Where birds do zing, below the zun,
In trees above the blue-smok'd tun,
An' sheades o' stems do overstratch
The mossy path 'ithin the hatch ;

If leaves be bright up over head,
   When May do shed its glitt'ren light :
Or, in the blight o' Fall, do spread
   A yollow bed avore our zight—
   Whatever season it mid be,
      The trees be always company.

When dusky night do nearly hide
The path along the hedge's zide,
An' dailight's hwomely sounds be still
But sounds o' water at the mill ;
Then if noo feace we long'd to greet
   Could come to meet our lwonesome treace ;
Or if noo peace o' weary veet,
   However fleet, could reach its pleace—
      However lwonesome we mid be,
      The trees would still be company.

38

CHILDHOOD

Aye, at that time our days wer but vew,
An' our lim's wer but small, an' a-growen ;
An' then the feair worold wer new,
An' life wer all hopevul an' gay ;
An' the times o' the sprouten o' leaves,
An' the cheak-burnen seasons o' mowen,
An' binden o' red-headed sheaves,
Wer all welcome seasons o' jay.

Then the housen seem'd high that be low,
An' the brook did seem wide that is narrow,
An' time, that do vlee, did goo slow,
An' veelens now feeble wer strong,
An' our worold did end wi' the neames
Ov the Sha'sbury Hill or Bulbarrow ;
An' life did seem only the geames
That we play'd as the days rolled along !

PENTRIDGE BY THE RIVER

Pentridge !—oh ! my heart's a-zwellen
Vull o' jay wi' vo'k a-tellen
   Any news o' thik wold pleace,
An' the boughy hedges round it,
An' the river that do bound it
   Wi' his dark but glis'nen feace.
Vor there's noo land, on either hand,
To me lik' Pentridge by the river.

Be there any leaves to quiver
On the aspen by the river ?
   Doo he sheade the water still,
Where the rushes be a-growen,
Where the sullen Stour's a-flowen
   Drough the meads vrom mill to mill ?
Vor if a tree wer dear to me,
Oh ! 'twer thik aspen by the river.

There, in eegrass new a-shooten,
I did run on even vooten,
   Happy, over new mown land ;
Or did zing wi' zingen drushes
While I plaited, out o' rushes,
   Little baskets vor my hand ;
Bezide the clote that there did float,
Wi' yollow blossoms, on the river.

When the western zun's a vallen,
What shrill vaice is now a-callen
  Hwome the deairy to the pails :
Who do dreve em on, a-flingen
Wide-bow'd horns, or slowly zwingen
  Right an' left their tufty tails ?
As they do goo a-huddled drough
The geate a-leaden up vrom river.

Bleaded grass is now a-shooten
Where the vloor wer woonce our vooten,
  While the hall wer still in pleace.
Stwones be looser in the wallen ;
Hollow trees be nearer vallen ;
  Ev'ry thing ha' chang'd its feace.
But still the neame do bide the seame—
'Tis Pentridge—Pentridge by the river.

Cutt Mill.
Hinton St. Mary

BOB THE FIDDLER

Oh ! Bob the fiddler is the pride
O' chaps an' maidens vur an' wide ;
They can't keep up a merry tide,
   But Bob is in the middle.
If merry Bob do come avore ye,
He'll zing a zong, or tell a story ;
But if you'd zee en in his glory,
   Jist let en have a fiddle.

Aye, let en tuck a crowd below
His chin, an' gi'e his vist a bow,
He'll dreve his elbow to an' fro',
   An' play what you do please.
At Maypolen, or feast, or feair,
His earm wull zet off twenty peair,
An' meake em dance the groun' dirt-beare,
   An' hop about lik' vlees.

Long life to Bob ! the very soul
O' me'th at merry feast an' pole ;
Vor when the crowd do leave his jowl,
   They'll all be in the dumps.
Zoo at the dance another year,
At *Shillinston* or *Haxelbur'*,
Mid Bob be there to meake em stir,
   In merry jigs, their stumps !

AUNT'S TANTRUMS

Why ees, aunt Anne's a little staid,
But kind an' merry, poor wold maid !
If we don't cut her heart wi' slights,
She'll zit an' put out things to rights,
Upon a hard day's work, o' night ;
    But zet her up, she's jis' lik' vier,
      An' woe betide the woone that's nigh 'er
        When she is in her tantrums.

She'll toss her head, a-steppen out
Such strides, an' fling the pails about ;
An' slam the doors as she do goo,
An' kick the cat out wi' her shoe,
Enough to het her off in two.
    The bwoys do bundle out o' house,
      A-lassen they should get a towse,
        When aunt is in her tantrums.

She whurr's, woone day, the wooden bowl
In such a veag at my poor poll ;
It brush'd the heair above my crown,
An' whizz'd on down upon the groun',
An' knock's the bantam cock right down ;
    But up he sprung, a-teaken flight
      Wi' tothers, clucken in a fright,
        Vrom aunt in such a tantrum !

But Dick stole in, an' reach'd en down
The biggest blather to be voun',
An' crope an' put en out o' zight
Avore the vire, an' plimm'd en tight
An crack'd en wi' the slice thereright.
  She screm'd, an' bundled out o' house,
  An' got so quiet as a mouse,—
    It frighten'd off her tantrum.

EASTER ZUNDAY

Last Easter Jim put on his blue
Frock cwoat, the vu'st time—vier new ;
Wi' yollow buttons all o' brass,
That glitter'd in the zun lik' glass ;
An' pok'd 'ithin the button-hole
A tutty he'd a-begg'd or stole.
A span-new wes-co't, too, he wore,
Wi' yollow stripes all down avore ;
An' tied his breeches' lags below
The knee, wi' ribbon in a bow ;
An' drow'd his kitty-boots azide,
An' put his laggens on, an' tied
His shoes wi' strings two vingers wide,
  Because 'twer Easter Zunday.

An' after mornen church wer out
He come back hwome, an' stroll'd about
All down the vields, an' drough the leane,
Wi' sister Kit an' cousin Jeane,
A-turnen proudly to their view
His yollow breast an' back o' blue.
The lambs did play, the grounds wer green,
The trees did bud, the zun did sheen ;
The lark did zing below the sky,
An' roads wer all a-blown so dry,
As if the zummer wer begun ;
An' he had sich a bit o' fun !
He meade the maidens squeal an' run,
  Because 'twer Easter Zunday.

THE GIRT WOAK TREE THAT'S IN THE DELL

The girt woak tree that's in the dell !
There's noo tree I do love so well ;
Vor times an' times when I wer young
I there've a-climb'd, an' there've a-zwung,
An' pick'd the eacorns green,a-shed
In wrestlen storms from his broad head,
An' down below's the cloty brook
Where I did vish with line an' hook,
An' beat, in playsome dips and zwims,
The foamy stream, wi' white-skinn'd lim's.
An' there my mother nimbly shot
Her knitten-needles, as she zot
At evenen down below the wide
Woak's head, wi' father at her zide.
An' I've a-played wi' many a bwoy,
That's now a man an' gone awoy ;
    Zoo I do like noo tree so well
    'S the girt woak tree that's in the dell.

An' there, in leater years, I roved
Wi' thik poor maid I fondly lov'd,—
The maid too feair to die so soon,—
When evenen twilight, or the moon,
Cast light enough 'ithin the pleace
To show the smiles upon her feace,

46

Wi' eyes so clear's the glassy pool,
An' lips an' cheaks so soft as wool.
There han' in han', wi' bosoms warm
Wi' love that burn'd but thought noo harm,
Below the wide-bough'd tree we past
The happy hours that went too vast ;
An' though she'll never be my wife,
She's still my leaden star o' life.
She's gone : an' she've a-left to me
Her token in the girt woak tree ;
  Zoo I do love noo tree so well
  'S the girt woak tree that's in the dell.

An' oh ! mid never ax nor hook
Be brought to spweil his steately look ;
Nor ever roun' his ribby zides
Mid cattle rub ther heairy hides ;
Nor pigs rout up his turf, but keep
His lwonesome sheade vor harmless sheep ;
An' let en grow, an' let en spread,
An' let en live when I be dead.
But oh ! if men should come an' vell
The girt woak tree that's in the dell,
An' build his planks 'ithin the zide
O' zome girt ship to plough the tide,
Then, life or death ! I'd goo to sea,
A-sailen wi' the girt woak tree :
An' I upon his planks would stand,
An' die a-fighten vor the land,—
The land so dear,—the land so free,—
The land that bore the girt woak tree ;
  Vor I do love noo tree so well
  'S the girt woak tree that's in the dell.

LYDLINCH BELLS

When skies wer peale wi' twinklen stars,
An' whislen air a-risen keen ;
An' birds did leave the icy bars
To vind, in woods, their mossy screen ;
When vrozen grass, as white's a sheet,
Did scrunchy sharp below our veet,
An' water, that did sparkle red
At zun-zet, wer a-vrozen dead ;
The ringers then did spend an hour
A-ringen changes up in tow'r ;
Vor Lydlinch bells be good vor sound,
An' liked by all the naighbours round.

An' while along the leafless boughs
O' ruslen hedges, win's did pass,
An' orts ov hay, a-left by cows,
Did russle on the vrozen grass,
An' maidens' pails, wi' all their work
A-done, did hang upon their vurk,
An' they, avore the fleamen brand,
Did teake their needle-work in hand,
The men did cheer their heart an hour
A-ringen changes up in tow'r ;
Vor Lydlinch bells be good vor sound,
An' liked by all the naighbours round.

48

There sons did pull the bells that rung
Their mothers' wedden peals avore,
The while their fathers led em young
An' blushen vrom the church's door,
An' still did cheem, wi' happy sound,
As time did bring the Zundays round,
An' call em to the holy pleace
Vor heav'nly gifts o' peace an' greace ;
An' vo'k did come, a-streamen slow
Along below the trees in row,
While they, in merry peals, did sound
The bells vor all the naighbours round.

An' when the bells, wi' changen peal,
Did smite their own vo'ks' window-peanes,
Their sof'en'd sound did often steal
Wi' west winds drough the Bagber leanes ;
Or, as the win' did shift, mid goo
Where woody Stock do nessle lew,
Or where the risen moon did light
The walls o' Thornhill on the height ;
An' zoo, whatever time mid bring
To meake their vive clear vaices zing,
Still Lydlinch bells wer good vor sound,
An' liked by all the naighbours round.

BLACKMWORE MAIDENS

The primrwose in the sheade do blow,
The cowslip in the zun,
The thyme upon the down do grow,
The clote where streams do run ;
An' where do pretty maidens grow
An' blow, but where the tow'r
Do rise among the bricken tuns,
In Blackmwore by the Stour.

If you could zee their comely gait,
An' pretty feaces' smiles,
A-trippen on so light o' waight,
An' steppen off the stiles ;
A-gwain to church, as bells do swing
An' ring within the tow'r,
You'd own the pretty maidens' pleace
Is Blackmwore by the Stour.

If you vrom Wimborne took your road,
To Stower or Paladore,
An' all the farmers' housen show'd
Their daughters at the door ;
You'd cry to bachelors at hwome—
' Here, come : 'ithin an hour
You'll vind ten maidens to your mind,
In Blackmwore by the Stour.'

An' if you look'd 'ithin their door,
To zee em in their pleace,
A-doen housework up avore
Their smilen mother's feace ;
You'd cry—' Why, if a man would wive
An' thrive, 'ithout a dow'r,
Then let en look en out a wife
In Blackmwore by the Stour.'

As I upon my road did pass
A school-house back in May,
There out upon the beaten grass
Wer maidens at their play ;
An' as the pretty souls did tweil
An' smile, I cried, ' The flow'r
O' beauty, then, is still in bud
In Blackmwore by the Stour.'

BE'MI'STER

Sweet Be'mi'ster, that bist a-bound
By green an' woody hills all round,
Wi' hedges, reachen up between
A thousan' vields o' zummer green,
Where elems' lofty heads do drow
Their sheades vor hay-meakers below,
An' wild hedge-flow'rs do charm the souls
O' maidens in their evenen strolls.

When I o' Zunday nights wi' Jeane
Do saunter drough a vield or leane,
Where elder-blossoms be a-spread
Above the eltrot's milk-white head,
An' flow'rs o' blackberries do blow
Upon the brembles, white as snow,
To be outdone avore my zight
By Jean's gay frock o' dazzlen white ;

Oh ! then there's nothen that's i'thout
Thy hills that I do ho about,—
Noo bigger pleace, noo gayer town,
Beyond thy sweet bells' dyen soun',
As they do ring, or strike the hour,
At evenen vrom thy wold red tow'r
No : shelter still my head, an' keep
My bwones when I do vall asleep !

52

A WITCH

There's thik wold hag, Moll Brown,
Look zee, jus' past !
I wish the ugly sly wold witch
Would tumble over into ditch ;
I woulden pull her out not very vast.
No, no.   I don't think she's a bit belied,
No, she's a witch, aye, Molly's evil-eyed.
Vor I do know o' many a withren blight
A-cast on vo'k by Molly's muttered spite ;
She did, woone time, a dreadvul deal o' harm
To Farmer Gruff's vo'k, down at Lower Farm.
Vor there, woone day, they happened to offend her,
An' not a little to their sorrow,
Because they woulden gi'e or lend her
Zome 'hat she come to bag or borrow ;
An' zoo, d'ye know, they soon begun to vind
That she'd a-left her evil wish behind.
She soon bewitch'd em, an' she had such pow'r,
That she did meake their milk an' eale turn zour,
An' addle all the aggs their vowls did lay ;
They coulden vetch the butter in the churn,
An' all the cheese begun to turn
Agean to curds an' whey ;
The little pigs, a-runnen wi' the zow,
Did zicken, zomehow, noobody knew how,
An' vall, an' turn their snouts toward the sky,

An' only gi'e woone little grunt, an' die ;
An' all the little ducks an' chicken
Wer death-struck out in yard a-picken
Their bits o' food, an' vell upon their head,
An' flapp'd their little wings an' dropp'd down dead.
They coulden fat the calves, they woulden thrive ;
They coulden seave their lambs alive ;
Their sheep wer all a-coath'd, or gi'ed noo wool ;
The hosses vell away to skin an' bwones,
An' got so weak they coulden pull
A half a peck o' stwones :
The dog got dead-alive an' drowsy,
The cat vell zick an' woulden mousy ;
An' every time the vo'k went up to bed,
They wer a-hag-rod till they wer half dead.
They us'd to keep her out o' house, 'tis true,
A-nailen up at door a hoss's shoe ;
An' I've a-heard the farmer's wife did try
To dawk a needle or a pin
In drough her wold hard wither'd skin,
An' draw her blood, a-comen by :
But she could never vetch a drap,
For pins would ply an' needles snap
Agean her skin ; an' that, in coo'se
Did meake the hag bewitch em woo'se.

THE BACHELOR

No ! I don't begrudge en his life,
   Nor his goold, nor his housen, nor lands ;
Teake all o't, an' gi'e me my wife,
   A wife's be the cheapest ov hands.
     Lie alwone ! sigh alwone ! die alwone !
       Then be vorgot.
     No ! I be content wi' my lot.

Ah ! where be the vingers so feair,
   Vor to pat en so soft on the feace,
To mend ev'ry stitch that do tear,
   An' keep ev'ry button in pleace ?
     Crack a-tore ! brack a-tore ! back a-tore !
       Buttons a-vled !
     Vor want ov a wife wi' her thread.

Ah ! where is the sweet-perty head
   That do nod till he's gone out o' zight ?
An' where be the two earms a-spread,
   To show en he's welcome at night ?
     Dine alwone ! pine alwone ! whine alwone !
       Oh ! what a life !
     I'll have a friend in a wife.

An' when vrom a meeten o' me'th
  Each husban' do lead hwome his bride,
Then he do slink hwome to his he'th,
  Wi' his earm a-hung down his cwold zide.
    Slinken on! blinken on! thinken on!
        Gloomy an' glum;
    Nothen but dullness to come.

An' when he do onlock his door,
  Do rumble as hollow's a drum,
An' the vearies a-hid roun' the vloor,
  Do grin vor to see en so glum.
    Keep alwone! sleep alwone! weep alwone
        There let en bide,
    I'll have a wife at my zide.

But when he's a-laid on his bed
  In a zickness, O, what wull he do!
Vor the hands that would lift up his head,
  An' sheake up his pillor anew.
    Ills to come! pills to come! bills to come!
        Noo soul to sheare
    The trials the poor wratch must bear.

THE SETTLE AN' THE GIRT WOOD VIRE

Ah! naighbour John, since I an' you
Wer youngsters ev'ry thing is new.
My father's vires were all o' logs
O' cleft-wood, down upon the dogs
Below our clavy, high an' brode
Enough to teake a cart an' lwoad,
Where big an' little all zot down
At bwoth zides an' bevore, all roun'.
An' when I zot among em, I
Could see all up agean the sky
Drough chimney, where our vo'k did hitch
The zalt-box an' the beacon-vlitch,
An' watch the smoke on out o' vier,
All up an' out o' tun, an' higher.
An' there wer beacon up on rack,
An' pleates an' dishes on the tack ;
An' roun' the walls wer hearbs a-stowed
In peapern bags, an' blathers blowed.
An' just above the clavy-bwoard
Wer father's spurs, an' gun, an' sword ;
An' there wer then, our gre'test pride,
The settle by the vier zide.
  Ah ! gi'e me, if I wer a squier,
  The settle an' the girt wood vier.

But they've a-wall'd up now i' bricks
The vier pleace vor dogs an' sticks,

An' only left, a little hole
To teake a little greate o' coal,
So small that only twos or drees
Can jist push in an' warm their knees.
An' then the carpets they do use
Ben't fit to tread wi' ouer shoes ;
An' chairs an' couches be so neat
You mussen teake em vor a seat :
They be so fine, that vo'k mus' pleace
All over em an outer cease
An' then the cover, when 'tis on,
Is still too fine to loll upon.
Ah ! gi'e me if I wer a squier,
The settle an' the girt wood vier.

58

I GOT TWO VIELDS

I got two vields, an' I don't ceare
What squire mid have a bigger sheare.
My little zummer-leaze do stratch
All down the hangen, to a patch
O' mead between a hedge an' rank
Ov elems, an' a river bank.
Where yollow clotes, in spreaden beds
O' floaten leaves, do lift their heads
By benden bulrushes an' zedge
A-swayen at the water's edge,
Below the withy that do spread
Athirt the brook his grey-leav'd head.
An' eltrot flowers, milky white,
Do catch the slanten evenen light ;
An' in the meaple boughs, along
The hedge, do ring the blackbird's zong ;
Or in the day, a-vleen drough
The leafy trees, the whoa'se gookoo
Do zing to mowers that do zet
Their zives on end, an' stan' to whet.
From my wold house among the trees
A leane do goo along the leaze
O' yollow gravel, down between
Two mossy banks vor ever green.
An' trees, a-hangen overhead,
Do hide a trinklen gully-bed,
A-cover'd by a bridge vor hoss
Or man a-voot to come across.
Zoo wi' my hwomestead, I don't ceare
What squire mid have a bigger sheare !

59

DON'T CEARE

At the feast, I do mind very well, all the vo'ks
    Wer a-took in a happeren storm,
But we chaps took the maidens, an' kept em wi' clokes
    Under shelter, all dry an' all warm ;
An' to my lot vell Jeane, that's my bride,
That did titter, a-hung at my zide ;
Zaid her aunt, " Why the vo'k 'ull talk finely o' you,"
An', cried she, " I don't ceare if they do."

When the time o' the feast wer agean a-come round,
    An' the vo'k wer a-gather'd woonce mwore,
Why she guess'd if she went there, she'd soon be a-vound
    An' a-took seafely hwome to her door.
Zaid her mother, " 'Tis sure to be wet."
Zaid her cousin, " 'T'ull rain by zunzet."
Zaid her aunt, " Why the clouds there do look black an'
        blue,"
An' zaid she, " I don't ceare if they do."

An' at last, when she own'd I mid meake her my bride,
    Vor to help me, an' sheare all my lot,
An' wi' faithvulness keep all her life at my zide,
    Though my way mid be happy or not,
Zaid her naighbours, " Why wedlock's a clog,
An' a wife's a-tied up lik' a dog."

Zaid her aunt, " You'll vind trials enough vor to rue,"
An' zaid she, " I don't ceare if I do."

———

Now she's married, an' still in the midst ov her tweils
　　She's as happy's the daylight is long,
She do goo out abroad wi' her feace vull o' smiles,
　　An' do work in the house wi' a zong.
An', zays woone, " She don't grieve, you can tell."
Zays another, " Why, don't she look well ! "
Zays her aunt, " Why the young vo'k do envy you two,"
An', zays she, " I don't ceare if they do."

Now vor me I can zing in my business abrode,
　　Though the storm do beat down on my poll,
There's a wife-brighten'd vier at the end o' my road,
　　An' her love vor the jay o' my soul.
Out o' door I wi' rogues mid be tried :
Out o' door be brow-beaten wi' pride ;
Men mid scowl out o' door, if my wife is but true—
Let em scowl, " I don't ceare if they do."

A BIT O' SLY COORTEN

(ECLOGUE)

John and Fanny

JOHN

Now, Fanny, 'tis too bad, you teazen maid !
How leate you be a'come !   Where have ye stay'd ?
How long you have a-meade me wait about !
I thought you werden gwain to come agean ;
I had a mind to goo back hwome agean.
This idden when you promis'd to come out.

FANNY

Now 'tidden any good to meake a row,
Upon my word, I cooden come till now.
Vor I've a-been kept in all day by mother,
At work about woone little job an' t'other.
If you do want to goo though, don't ye stay
Vor me a minute longer, I do pray.

JOHN

I thought ye mid be out wid Jemmy Bleake.

FANNY

An' why be out wi' him, vor goodness' sake ?

JOHN

You walk'd o' Zunday evenen wi'n, d'ye know,
You went vrom church a-hitch'd up in his earm.

FANNY

Well, if I did, that werden any harm.
Lauk ! that *is* zome'at to teake notice o'

JOHN

He took ye roun' the middle at the stile,
An' kiss'd ye twice 'ithin the ha'f a mile.

FANNY

Ees, at the stile, because I shoulden vall,
He took me hold to help me down, that's all ;
An' I can't zee what very mighty harm
He could ha' done a-lenden me his earm.
An' as vor kissen o' me, if he did,
I didden ax en to, nor zay he mid :
An' if he kiss'd me dree times, or a dozen,
What harm wer it ?   Why iden he my cousin ?
An' I can't zee, then, what there is amiss
In Cousin Jem's jist gi'en me a kiss.

JOHN

Well, he shan't kiss ye, then ; you shan't be kiss'd
By his girt ugly chops, a lanky houn' !
If I do zee'n, I'll jist wring up my vist
An' knock en down.
I'll squot his girt pug-nose, if I don't miss en ;
I'll warn I'll spweil his pretty lips vor kissen !

FANNY

Well, John, I'm sure I little thought to vind
That you had ever sich a jealous mind.
What then ! I s'pose that I must be a dummy,
An' mussen goo about nor wag my tongue
To any soul, if he's a man, an' young ;
Or else you'll work yourzelf up mad wi' passion,

63

An' talk away o' gi'en vo'k a drashen,
An' breaken bwones, an' beaten heads to pummy !
If you've a-got sich jealous ways about ye,
I'm sure I should be better off 'ithout ye.

JOHN

Well, if girt Jemmy have a-won your heart,
We'd better break the coortship off, an' peart.

FANNY

He won my heart! There, John, don't talk sich stuff ;
Don't talk noo mwore, vor you've a-zaid enough.
If I'd a-liked another mwore than you,
I'm sure I shoulden come to meet ye zoo ;
Vor I've a-twold to father many a story,
An' took o' mother many a scwolden for ye.
(weeping)
But 'twull be over now, vor you shan't zee me
Out wi' ye noo mwore, to pick a quarrel wi' me !

JOHN

Well, Fanny, I woon't zay noo mwore, my dear.
Let's meake it up. Come, wipe off thik there tear.
Let's goo an zit o' top o' thease here stile,
An' rest, an' look about a little while.

FANNY

Now goo away, you crabbed jealous chap !
You shan't kiss me,—you shan't ! I'll gi' ye a slap.

JOHN

Then you look smilen ; don't you pout an' toss
Your head so much, an' look so very cross.

FANNY

Now, John ! don't squeeze me roun' the middle zoo.

I woon't stop here noo longer, if you do.
Why, John! be quiet, wull ye?   Fie upon it!
Now zee how you've a-rumpl'd up my bonnet!
Mother 'ill zee it after I'm at hwome,
An' gi'e a guess directly how it come.

JOHN
Then don't you zay that I be jealous, Fanny.

FANNY
I wull: vor you *be* jealous, Mister Jahnny.
There's zomebody a-comen down the groun'
Towards the stile.   Who is it?   Come, get down.
I must run hwome, upon my word then, now;
If I do stay, they'll kick up sich a row.
Good night.   I can't stay now.

JOHN
Then good night, Fanny!
Come out a-bit to morrow evenen, can ye?

VELLEN THE TREE

Aye, the girt elem tree out in little hwome groun'
Wer a-stannen this mornen, an' now's a-cut down.
Aye, the girt elem tree, so big roun' an' so high,
Where the mowers did goo to their drink, an' did lie
In the sheade ov his head, when the zun at his
heighth
Had a-drove em vrom mowen, wi' het an' wi' drith,
Where the hay-meakers put all their picks an' their
reakes
An' did squot down to snabble their cheese an'
their ceakes
An' did vill vrom their flaggons their cups wi' their
eale,
An' did meake theirzelves merry wi' joke an' wi'
teale.

Ees, we took up a rwope an' we tied en all round
At the top o'n, wi' woone end a-hangen to ground,
An' we cut, near the ground, his girt stem a'most
drough,
An' we bent the wold head o'n wi' woone tug or two ;
An' he sway'd all his limbs, an' he nodded his head,
Till he vell away down like a pillar o' lead :
An' as we did run vrom en, there, clwose at our
backs,

Oh ! his boughs come to groun' wi' sich whizzes an'
    cracks ;
An' his top wer so lofty that, now's a-vell down,
The stem o'n do reach a-most over the groun'.

Zoo the girt elem tree out in little hwome groun'
Wer a-stannen this mornen, an' now's a-cut down.

JOHN BLOOM IN LON'ON
[*all true*]

John Bloom he wer a jolly soul,
    A grinder o' the best o' meal,
Bezide a river that did roll,
    Vrom week to week, to push his wheel.
His flour wer all a-meade o' wheat ;
An' fit for bread that vo'k mid eat ;
Vor he would starve avore he'd cheat.
" 'Tis pure," woone woman cried ;
" Aye, sure," woone mwore replied ;
" You'll vind it nice. Buy woonce, buy twice,"
Cried worthy Bloom the miller.

Athirt the chest he wer so wide
    As two or dree òv me or you.
An' wider still vrom zide to zide,
    An' I do think still thicker drough.
Vall down, he coulden, he did lie
When he wer up on-zide so high
As up on-end or perty nigh.
" Meake room," woone naighbour cried ;
" 'Tis Bloom," woone mwore replied ;
" Good morn t'ye all, bwoth girt an' small,"
Cried worthy Bloom the miller.

Noo stings o' conscience ever broke
    His rest, a-twiten o'n wi' wrong,

68

Zoo he did sleep till mornen broke,
    An' birds did call en wi' their zong.
But he did love a harmless joke,
An' love his evenen whiff o' smoke,
A-zitten in his cheair o' woak.
" Your cup," his daughter cried ;
" Vill'd up," his wife replied ;
" Aye, aye ; a drap avore my nap,"
Cried worthy Bloom the miller.

When Lon'on vok did meake a show
    O' their girt glassen house woone year,
An' people went, bwoth high an' lo,
    To zee the zight, vrom vur an' near,
" O well," cried Bloom, "why I've a right
So well's the rest to zee the zight ;
I'll goo, an' teake the rail outright."
" Your feare," the booker cried ;
" There, there," good Bloom replied ;
" Why this June het do meake woone zweat,"
Cried worthy Bloom the miller,

Then up the guard did whissle sh'ill,
    An' then the engine pank'd a-blast,
An' rottled on so loud's a mill,
    Avore the train, vrom slow to vast.
An' oh ! at last how they did spank
By cutten deep, an' high-cast bank
The while their iron ho'se did pank.
" Do whizzy," woone o'm cried ;
" I'm dizzy," woone replied ;
" Aye's, here's the road to hawl a lwoad,"
Cried worthy Bloom the miller.

In Lon'on John zent out to call
   A tidy trap, that he mid ride
To zee the glassen house, an' all
   The lot o' things a-stow'd inside.
" Here, Boots, come here," cried he, " I'll dab
A sixpence in your han' to nab
Down street a tidy little cab."
" A feare," the boots then cried ;
" I'm there," the man replied.
" The glassen pleace, your quickest peace,"
Cried worthy Bloom the miller.

The steps went down wi' rottlen slap,
   The zwingen door went open wide :
Wide ? no ; vor when the worthy chap
   Stepp'd up to teake his pleace inside,
Breast-foremost, he wer twice too wide
Vor thik there door.   An' then he tried
To edge in woone an' t'other zide.
" 'Twon't do," the drever cried ;
" Can't goo," good Bloom replied ;
" That you should bring thease vooty thing ! "
Cried worthy Bloom the miller.

" Come," cried the drever.   " Pay your feare
   You'll teake up all my time, good man."
" Well," answer'd Bloom, "to meake that square,
   You teake up me, then, if you can."
" I come at call," the man did nod.
" What then ? " cried Bloom, " I han't a-rod,
An' can't in thik there hodmadod."
" Girt lump," the drever cried ;
" Small stump," good Bloom replied ;

70

" A little mite, to meake so light,
O' jolly Bloom the miller."

" You'd best be off now perty quick,"
  Cried Bloom, "an vind a lighter lwoad,
Or else I'll vetch my voot, an' kick
  The vooty thing athirt the road."
" Who is the man ? " they cried, "meake room,"
" A halfstarv'd Do'set man," cried Bloom ;
" You be ? " another cried ;
" Hee ! Hee ! " woone mwore replied.
" Aye, shrunk so thin, to bwone an' skin,"
Cried worthy Bloom the miller.

MY ORCHA'D IN LINDEN LEA

'Ithin the woodlands, flow'ry gleaded,
　　By the woak tree's mossy moot,
The sheenen grass-bleades, timber-sheaded,
　　Now do quiver under voot ;
An' birds do whissle over head,
An' water's bubblen in its bed,
An' there vor me the apple tree
Do lean down low in Linden Lea.

When leaves that leately wer a-springen
　　Now do feade 'ithin the copse,
An' painted birds do hush their zingen
　　Up upon the timber's tops ;
An' brown-leav'd fruit's a-turnen red,
In cloudless zunsheen, over head,
Wi' fruit vor me, the apple tree
Do lean down low in Linden Lea.

Let other vo'k meake money vaster
　　In the air o' dark-room'd towns,
I don't dread a peevish measter ;
　　Though noo man do heed my frowns,
I be free to goo abrode,
Or teake agean my hwomeward road
To where, vor me, the apple tree
Do lean down low in Linden Lea.

72

THE SHY MAN

Ah ! good Measter Gwillet, that you mid ha' know'd,
Wer a-bred up at Coomb, an' went little abroad ;
An' if he got in among strangers, he velt
His poor heart in a twitter, an' ready to melt ;
Or if, by ill luck, in his rambles, he met
Wi' zome maidens a-titt'ren, he burn'd wi' a het,
That shot all drough the lim's o'n, an' left a cwold
   zweat,
  The poor little chap wer so shy,
  He wer ready to drap, an' to die.

But at last 'twer the lot o' the poor little man
To vall deeply in love, as the best ov us can ;
An' 'twer noo easy task vor a shy man to tell
Sich a dazzlen feair maid that he loved her so well ;
An' woone day when he met her, his knees nearly
   smote
Woone another, an' then wi' a struggle he brote
A vew words to his tongue, wi' some mwore in his
   droat.
  But she, 'ithout doubt, could soon vind
  Vrom two words that come out, zix behind.

Zoo at langth, when he vound her so smilen an' kind,
Why he wrote her zome lains, vor to tell her his
   mind,

Though 'twer then a hard task vor a man that wer
　　　shy,
To be married in church, wi' a crowd stannen by.
But he twold her woone day, ' I have housen an'
　　　lands,
We could marry by licence, if you don't like banns ' ;
An' he cover'd his eyes up wi' woone ov his han's,
　　　Vor his head seem'd to zwim as he spoke,
　　　An' the air look'd so dim as a smoke.

Well ! he vound a good naighbour to goo in his pleace
Vor to buy the goold ring, vor he hadden the feace.
An' when he went up vor to put in the banns,
He did sheake in his lags, an' did sheake in his han's.
Then they ax'd vor her neame, an' her parish or
　　　town,
An' he gi'ed em a leaf, wi' her neame a-wrote down ;
Vor he coulden ha' twold em outright vor a poun'.
　　　Vor his tongue wer so weak an' so loose,
　　　When he wanted to speak 'twer noo use.

Zoo they went to be married, an' when they got
　　　there
All the vo'k wer a-gather'd as if 'twer a feair,
An' he thought, though his pleace mid be pleasant
　　　to zome,
He could all but ha' wish'd that he hadden a-come.
The bride wer a-smilen as fresh as a rwose,
An' when he come wi' her, an' show'd his poor nose,
All the little bwoys shouted, an' cried ' There he
　　　goes,
　　　There he goes.'　Oh ! vor his peart he velt
　　　As if the poor heart o'n would melt.

74

An' when they stood by the chancel together,
Oh ! a man mid ha' knock'd en right down wi' a
    veather,
He did veel zoo asheam'd that he thought he would
    rather
He werden the bridegroom, but only the father.
But, though 'tis so funny to zee en so shy,
Yet his mind is so lowly, his aims be so high,
That to do a mean deed, or to tell woone a lie,
    You'd vind that he'd shun mwore by half
    Than to stan' vor vo'ks fun, or their laugh.

THE BEST MAN IN THE VIELD
(ECLOGUE)

Sam and Bob

SAM

That's slowish work, Bob.   What'st a-been about ?
Thy pooken don't goo on not over sprack.
Why I've a-pook'd my weale, lo'k zee, clear out,
An' here I be agean a-turnen back.

BOB

I'll work wi' thee then, Sammy, any day,
At any work dost like to teake me at,
Vor any money thou dost like to lay.
Now, Mister Sammy, what dost think o' that ?
My weale is nearly twice so big as thine,
Or else, I warnt, I shouldden be behin'.

SAM

Ah ! hang thee, Bob ! don't tell sich whoppen lies.
My weale's the biggest, if do come to size.
'Tis jist the seame whatever bist about ;
Why, when dost goo a-tedden grass, you sloth,
Another hand's a-fwoc'd to teake thy zwath,
An' ted a half way back to help thee out ;
An' then a-reaken rollers, bist so slack,
Dost keep the very bwoys an' women back.

An' if dost think that thou canst challenge I
At any thing,—then, Bob, we'll teake a pick a-piece,
An' woonce thease zummer, goo an' try
To meake a rick a-piece.
A rick o' thine wull look a little funny,
When thou'st a-done en, I'll bet any money.

BOB

You noggerhead ! last year thou mead'st a rick,
An' then we had to trig en wi' a stick.
An' what did John that tipp'd en zay ? Why zaid
He stood a-top o'en all the while in dread,
A-thinken that avore he should a-done en
He'd tumble over slap wi' him upon en.

SAM

You yoppen dog ! I warnt I meade my rick
So well's thou mead'st thy lwoad o' hay last week.
They hadden got a hundred yards to haul en,
An' then they vound 'twer best to have en boun',
Vor if they hadden, 'twould a-tumbl'd down ;
An' after that I zeed en all but vallen,
An' trigg'd en up wi' woone o'm's pitchen pick,
To zee if I could meake en ride to rick ;
An' when they had the dumpy heap unboun',
He vell to pieces flat upon the groun'.

BOB

Do shut thy lyen chops ! What dosten mind
Thy pitchen to me out in Gully-plot,
A-meaken o' me wait (wast zoo behind)
A half an hour vor ev'ry pitch I got ?
An' how didst groun' thy pick ? an' how didst quirk

To get en up on end ?   Why hadst hard work
To rise a pitch that wer about so big
'S a goodish crow's nest, or a wold man's wig !
Why bist so weak, dost know, as any roller :
Zome o' the women vo'k will beat thee hollor.

SAM

You snub-nos'd flopperchops !   I pitch'd so quick,
That thou dost know thou hadst a hardish job
To teake in all the pitches off my pick ;
An' dissen zee me groun' en, nother, Bob.
An' thou bist stronger, thou dost think, than I ?
Girt bandy-lags !   I jist should like to try.
We'll goo, if thou dost like, an' jist zee which
Can heave the mwost, or car the biggest nitch.

BOB

There, Sam, do meake me zick to hear thy braggen !
Why bissen strong enough to car a flagon.

SAM

You grinnen fool ! why I'd zet thee a-blowen,
If thou wast wi' me vor a day a-mowen.
I'd wear my cwoat, an' thou midst pull thy rags off,
An' then in half a zwath I'd mow thy lags off.

BOB

Thee mow wi' me !   Why coossen keep up wi' me :
Why bissen fit to goo a-vield to skimmy,
Or mow down docks an' thistles !   Why I'll bet
A shillen, Samuel, that thou cassen whet.

SAM

Now don't thee zay much mwore than what'st a-zaid,
Or else I'll knock thee down, heels over head.

BOB

Thou knock me down, indeed ! Why cassen gi'e
A blow half hard enough to kill a bee.

SAM

Well, thou shalt veel upon thy chops and snout.

BOB

Come on, then Samel ; jist let's have woone bout.

IN THE SPRING

My love is the maid ov all maidens,
  Though all mid be comely,
Her skin's lik' the jessamy blossom
  A-spread in the Spring.

Her smile is so sweet as a beaby's
  Young smile on his mother,
Her eyes be as bright as the dew drop
  A-shed in the Spring.

O grey-leafy pinks o' the gearden,
  Now bear her sweet blossoms ;
Now deck wi' a rwose bud, O briar,
  Her head in the Spring.

O ligh-rollen wind, blow me hither
  The vaice ov her talken,
O bring vrom her veet the light doust
  She do tread in the Spring.

O zun, meake the gil'cups all glitter
  In goold all around her,
An' meake o' the deaisys' white flowers
  A bed in the Spring.

O whissle, gay birds, up bezide her,
  In drong-way an' woodlands,

O zing, swingen lark, now the clouds
    Be a-vled in the Spring !

An' who, you mid ax, be my praises
    A-meaken so much o'
An' oh ! 'tis the maid I'm a-hopen
    To wed in the Spring.

VULL A MAN

No, I'm a man, I'm vull a man,
You beat my manhood, if you can.
You'll be a man if you can teake
All steates that household life do meake.
The love-toss'd child, a-croodlen loud,
    The bwoy a-screamen wild in play,
The tall grown youth a-steppen proud,
    The father staid, the house's stay.
        No ; I can boast if others can,
            I'm vull a man.

A young-cheak'd mother's tears mid vall,
When woone a-lost, not half man-tall,
Vrom little hand, a-called vrom play,
Do leave noo tool, but drop a tay,
An' die avore he's father-free
    To sheape his life by his own plan ;
An' vull an angel he shall be,
    But here on e'th not vull a man,
        No ; I could boast if others can,
            I'm vull a man.

I woonce, a child, wer father-fed,
An' I've a-vound my childern bread ;
My earm, a sister's trusty crook,
Is now a faithvul wife's own hook ;

An' I've a-gone where vo'k did zend,
  An' gone upon my own free mind,
An' of'en at my own wits' end.
  A-led o' God while I were blind.
    No ; I could boast if others can
      I'm vull a man.

An' still, ov all my tweil ha' won,
My loven maid an' merry son,
Though each in turn's a jay an' ceare,
'Ve a-had, an' still shall have, their sheare ;
An' then, if God should bless their lives,
  Why I mid zend vrom son to son
My life, right on drough men an' wives,
  As long, good now, as time do run.
    No ; I could boast if others can,
      I'm vull a man.

NANNY GILL

Ah ! they wer times, when Nanny Gill
Went so'jeren ageanst her will,
  Back when the King come down to view
His ho'se an' voot, in red an' blue,
    An' they did march in rows,
    An' wheel in lines an' bows,
    Below the King's own nose ;
An' guns did pwoint, an' swords did gleare,
A-fighten foes that werden there.

Poor Nanny Gill did goo to zell
In town her glitt'ren macarel,
A-pack'd wi' ceare, in even lots,
A-ho'seback in a peair o' pots.
    An' zoo when she did ride
    Between her panniers wide,
    Red-cloked in all her pride,
Why, who but she, an' who but broke
The road avore her scarlet cloke !

But Nanny's ho'se that she did ride,
Woonce carr'd a sword agean his zide,
An' had, to prick en into rank,
A so'jer's spurs agean his flank ;
    An' zoo, when he got zight
    O' swords a-gleamen bright,
    An' men agwain to fight,
He set his eyes athirt the ground,
An' prick'd his ears to catch the sound.

Then Nanny gi'ed his zide a kick,
An' het en wi' her limber stick ;
But suddenly a horn did sound,
An' zend the ho'semen on vull bound ;
   An' her ho'se at the zight
   Went after em, vull flight,
   Wi' Nanny in a fright,
A-pullen, wi' a scream an' grin,
Her wold brown rains to hold en in.

But no ! he went away vull bound,
As vast as he could tear the ground,
An' took, in line, a so'jer's pleace,
Vor Nanny's cloke an' frighten'd feace ;
   While vo'k did laugh an' shout
   To zee her cloke stream out,
   As she did wheel about,
A-cryen, " Oh ! la ! dear ! " in fright,
The while her ho'se, did play sham fight.

85

VO'K A-COMEN INTO CHURCH

The church do zeem a touchen zight,
　When vo'k, a-comen in at door,
　Do softly tread the long-ail'd vloor
Below the pillar'd arches' height,
　　Wi' bells a-pealen,
　　Vo'k a-kneelen,
Hearts a-healen, wi' the love
An' peace a-zent em vrom above.

An' there, wi' mild an' thoughtvul feace,
　Wi' downcast eyes, an' vaices dum',
　The wold an' young do slowly come,
An' teake in stillness each his pleace,
　　A-zinken slowly,
　　Kneelen lowly,
Seeken holy thoughts alwone,
In pray'r avore their Meaker's thrcne.

An' there be sons in youthvul pride,
　An' fathers weak wi' years an' pain,
　An' daughters in their mother's train,
The tall wi' smaller at their zide ;
　　Heads in murnen
　　Never turnen,
Cheaks a-burnen, wi' the het
O' youth, an' eyes noo tears do wet.

There friends do settle, zide by zide,
　The knower speechless to the known ;
　Their vaice is there vor God alwone
To flesh an' blood their tongues be tied.
　　Grief a-wringen,
　　Jay a-zingen,
Pray'r a-bringen welcome rest
So softly to the troubled breast.

CULVER DELL AND THE SQUIRE

There's noo pleace I do like so well,
As Elem Knap in Culver Dell,
Where timber trees, wi' lofty shouds,
Did rise avore the western clouds ;
An' stan' agean, wi' veathery tops,
A-swayen up in North-Hill Copse.
An' on the east the mornen broke
Above a dewy grove o' woak ;
An' noontide shed its burnen light
On ashes on the southern height ;
An' I could vind zome teales to tell,
O' former days in Culver Dell.

A'n all the vo'k did love so well
The good wold squire o' Culver Dell,
That used to ramble drough the sheades
O' timber, or the burnen gleades,
An' come at evenen up the leaze
Wi' red-ear'd dogs bezide his knees ;
An' hold his gun, a-hangen drough
His earmpit, out above his tooe,
Wi' kindly words upon his tongue
Vor vo'k that met en, wold an' young ;
Vor he did know the poor so well
'S the richest vo'k in Culver Dell.

An' while the woak, wi' spreaden head,
Did sheade the foxes' verny bed ;
An' runnen heares, in zunny gleades,

Did beat the grasses' quiv'ren' bleades;
An' speckled pa'tridges took flight
In stubble vields a-feaden white ;
Or he could zee the pheasant strut
In sheady woods, wi' painted cwoat ;
Or long-tongued dogs did love to run
Among the leaves, bezide his gun ;
We didden want vor call to dwell
At hwome in peace in Culver Dell.

But now I hope his kindly feace
Is gone to vind a better pleace ;
But still, wi' vo'k a-left behind
He'll always be a-kept in mind
Vor all his springy-vooted hounds
Ha' done o' trotten round his grounds,
An' we have all a-left the spot,
To teake, a-scatter'd, each his lot ;
An' even Father, lik' the rest,
Ha' left our long vorseaken nest ;
An' we should vind it sad to dwell
Agean at hwome in Culver Dell.

The airy mornens still mid smite
Our windows wi' their rwosy light,
An' high-zunn'd noons mid dry the dew
On growen groun' below our shoe ;
The blushen evenen still mid dye
Wi' viry red the western sky ;
The zunny spring-time's quicknen power
Mid come to open leaf an' flower ;
An' days an' tides mid bring us on
Woone pleasure when another's gone.
But we must bid a long farewell
To days an' tides in Culver Dell.

I

FATHERHOOD

Let en zit, wi' his dog an' his cat,
 Wi' their noses a-turn'd to the vier,
 An' have all that a man should desire ;
But there idden much readship in that.
Whether vo'k mid have childern or no,
 Wou'dden meake mighty odds in the main ;
They do bring us mwore jay wi' mwore ho,
 An' wi' nwone we've less jay wi' less pain.
We be all lik' a zull's idle sheare out,
An' shall rust out, unless we do wear out,
 Lik' do-nothen, rue-nothen,
  Dead alive dumps.

As vor me, why my life idden bound
 To my own heart alwone, among men ;
 I do live in myzelf, an' agean
In the lives o' my childern all round :
I do live wi' my bwoy in his play,
 An' agean wi' my maid in her zongs ;
An' my heart is a-stirr'd wi' they jay,
 An' would burn at the zight o' their wrongs.
I ha' nine lives, an' zoo if a half
O'm do cry, why the rest o'm mid laugh
 All so playvully, jayvully,
  Happy wi' hope.

Tother night I come hwome a long road,
 When the weather did sting an' did vreeze ;
An' the snow—vor the day had a-snow'd—

90

Wer avroze on the boughs o' the trees ;
An' my tooes an' my vingers wer num',
  An' my veet we so lumpy as logs,
An' my ears wer so red's a cock's cwom, ;
  An' my nose wer so cwold as a dog's ;
But so soon's I got hwome I vorgot
Where my limbs wer a-cwold or wer hot,
  When wi' loud cries an' proud cries
      They coll'd me so cwold.

Vor the vu'st that I happen'd to meet
  Come to pull my girtcwoat vrom my earm,
  An' another did rub my feace warm,
An' another hot-slipper'd my veet ;
While their mother did cast on a stick,
  Vor to keep the red vier alive ;
An' they all come so busy an' thick
  As the bees vlee-en into their hive,
An' they meade me so happy an' proud,
That my heart could ha' crow'd out a-loud ;
  They did tweil zoo, an' smile zoo,
      An' coll me so cwold.

As I zot wi' my teacupt, at rest,
  There I pull'd out the tays I did bring ;
  Men a-kicken, a-wagg'd wi' a string,
An' goggle-ey'd dolls to be drest ;
An' oh ! vrom the childern there sprung
  Such a charm when they handled their tays,
That vor pleasure the bigger woones wrung
  Their two hands at the zight o' their jays ;
As the bwoys' bigger vaices vell in
Wi' the maidens a-titteren thin,
  An' their dancen an' prancen,
      An' little mouth's laughs.

Though 'tis hard stripes to breed em all up,
　　If I'm only a-blest vrom above,
　　They'll meake me amends wi' their love,
Vor their pillow, their pleate, an' their cup ;
Though I shall be never a-spweil'd
　　Wi' the sarvice that money can buy ;
Still the hands ov a wife an' a child
　　Be the blessens ov low or ov high ;
An' if there be mouths to be ved,
He that zent em can zend me their bread,
　　An' will smile on the chile
　　　　That's a-new on the knee.

GAMMONY GAY

Oh ! thik Gammony Gay is so droll,
That if he's at hwome by the he'th,
Or wi' vo'k out o' door, he's the soul
O' the meeten vor antics an' me'th ;
He do cast off the thoughts ov ill luck
As the water's a-shot vrom a duck ;
He do zing where his naighbours would cry—
He do laugh where the rest o's would sigh :
Noo other's so merry o' feace,
In the pleace, as Gammony Gay.

An' o' worken days, oh ! he do wear
Such a funny roun' hat,—you mid know't—
Wi' a brim all a-strout roun' his heair,
An' his glissenen eyes down below't ;
An' a cwoat wi' broad skirts that do vlee
In the wind ov his walk, round his knee ;
An' a peair o' girt pockets lik' bags,
That do swing an' do bob at his lags :
While me'th do walk out drough the pleace,
In the feace o' Gammony Gay.

An' if he do goo over groun'
Wi' noo soul vor to greet wi' his words,
The feace o'n do look up an' down,
An' round en so quick as a bird's ;

93

An' if he do vall in wi' vo'k,
Why, tidden vor want ov a joke,
If he don't zend em on vrom the pleace
Wi' a smile or a grin on their feace :
An' the young wi' the wold have a-heard
A kind word vrom Gammony Gay.

An' when he do whissel or hum,
'Ithout thinken o' what he's a-doen,
He'll beat his own lags vor a drum,
An' bob his gay head to the tuen ;
An' then you mid zee, 'etween whiles,
His feace all alive wi' his smiles,
An' his gay-breathen bozom do rise,
An' his me'th do sheen out ov his eyes :
An' at last to have praise or have bleame
Is the seame to Gammony Gay.

All the house-dogs do waggle their tails
If they do but catch zight ov his feace ;
An' the hosses do look over rails,
An' do whicker to zee'n at the pleace ;
An' he'll always bestow a good word
On a cat or a whisselen bird ;
An' even if culvers do coo,
Or an' owl is a-cryen ' Hoo, hoo,'
Where he is, there's always a joke
To be spoke, by Gammony Gay.

OUR FATHERS' WORKS

Ah ! I do think, as I do tread
Thease path, wi' elems overhead,
A-climen slowly up vrom Bridge,
By easy steps, to Broadwoak Ridge,
That all thease roads that we do bruise
Wi' hosses' shoes, or heavy lwoads ;
An' hedges' bands, where trees in row
Do rise an' grow aroun' the lands,
Be works that we've a-vound a-wrought
By our vorefathers' ceare an' thought.

They clear'd the groun' vor grass to teake
The pleace that bore the bremble breake,
An' drain'd the fen, where water spread,
A-lyen dead, a beane to men ;
An' built the mill, where still the wheel
Do grind our meal, below the hill ;
An' turn'd the bridge, wi' arch a-spread,
Below a road, vor us to tread.

They vound a pleace, where we mid seek
The gifts o' greace vrom week to week ;
An' built wi' stwone, upon the hill,
A tow'r we still do call our own ;
With bells to use, an' meake rejaice,
Wi' giant vaice, at our good news :
An' lifted stwones an' beams to keep
The rain an' cwold vrom us asleep.

Zoo now mid nwone ov us vorget
The pattern our vorefathers zet ;
But each be fain to underteake
Some work to meake vor others' gain,
That we mid leave mwore good to sheare,
Less ills to bear, less souls to grieve,
An' when our hands do vall to rest,
It mid be vrom a work a-blest.

'An' turned the bridge ------

Town Bridge, Sturminster Newton

THE SLANTEN LIGHT O' FALL

Ah ! Jeane, my maid, I stood to you,
   When you wer christen'd, small an' light,
Wi' tiny earms o' red an' blue,
   A-hangen in your robe o' white.
We brought ye to the hallow'd stwone,
Vor Christ to teake ye vor his own,
When harvest work wer all a-done,
An' time brought round October zun—
     The slanten light o' Fall.

An' I can mind the wind wer rough,
   An' gather'd clouds, but brought noo storms,
An' you did nessle warm enough,
   'Ithin your smilen mother's earms.
The whindlen grass did quiver light,
Among the stubble, feaded white,
An' if at times the zunlight broke
Upon the ground, or on the vo'k,
     'Twer slanten light o' Fall.

An' when we brought ye drough the door
   O' Knapton Church, a child o' greace,
There cluster'd round a'most a score
   O' vo'k to zee your tiny feace.
An' there we all did veel so proud,
To zee an' op'nen in the cloud,
An' then a stream o' light break drough,
A-sheenen brightly down on you—
     The slanten light o' Fall.

But now your time's a-come to stand
  In church, a-blushen at my zide,
The while a bridegroom vrom my hand
  Ha' took ye vor his faithvul bride.
Your christen neame we gi'd ye here,
When Fall did cool the weasten year;
An' now, agean, we brought ye drough
The doorway, wi' your surneame new,
    In slanten light o' Fall.

An' zoo vur, Jeane, your life is feair,
  An' God ha' been your steadvast friend,
An' mid ye have mwore jay than ceare,
  Vor ever, till your journeys end.
An' I've a-watch'd ye on wi' pride,
But now I soon mus' leave your zide,
Vor you ha' still life's spring-tide zun,
But my life, Jeane, is now a-run
    To slanten light o' Fall.

THE VIER-ZIDE

'Tis zome vo'ks jay to teake the road,
An' goo abro'd, a-wand'ren wide,
Vrom shere to shere, vrom pleace to pleace,
The swiftest peace that vo'k can ride.
But I've a jay 'ithin the door,
Wi' friends avore the vier-zide.

An' zoo, when winter skies do lour,
An' when the Stour's a-rollen wide,
Drough bridge-voot rails, a-painted white,
To be at night the traveller's guide,
Gi'e me a pleace that's warm an' dry,
A-zitten nigh my vier-zide.

If, when a friend ha' left the land,
I shook his hand a-most wet-eyed,
I velt too well the op'nen door
Would lead noo mwore where he did bide,
An' where I heard his vaice's sound,
In me'th around the vier-zide.

As I've a-zeed how vast do vall
The mwold'ren hall, the wold vo'ks pride,
Where merry hearts wer woonce a-ved
Wi' daily bread, why, I've a-sigh'd
To zee the wall so green wi' mwold,
An' vind so cwold the vier-zide.

An' Chris'mas still mid bring his me'th
To ouer he'th, but if we tried
To gather all that woonce did wear
Gay feaces there !   Ah ! zome ha' died,
An' zome be gone to leave wi' gaps
O' missen laps, the vier-zide.

But come now, bring us in your hand
A heavy brand o' woak a-dried,
To cheer us wi' his het an' light,
While vrosty night, so starry-skied,
Do gather souls that time do speare
To zit an' sheare our vier-zide.

CHRISTMAS INVITATION

Come down to-morrow night ; an' mind,
Don't leave thy fiddle-bag behind ;
We'll sheake a lag, 'an drink a cup
O' eale, to keep wold Chris'mas up.

You won't meet any stranger's feace,
But only naighbours o' the pleace,
An' Stowe, an' Combe ; an' two or dree
Vrom uncle's up at Rookery.

An' thou wu'lt vind a rwosy feace,
An' peair ov eyes so black as sloos,
The prettiest woones in all the pleace,—
I'm sure I needen tell thee whose.

We got a back-bran', dree girt logs
So much as dree ov us can car ;
We'll put em up athirt the dogs,
An' meake a vier to the bar.

An' ev'ry woone shall tell his teale,
An' ev'ry woone shall zing his zong,
An' ev'ry woone wull drink his eale
To love an' frien'ship all night long.

We'll snap the tongs, we'll have a ball,
We'll sheake the house, we'll lift the ruf,
We'll romp an' meake the maidens squall,
A catchen o'm at blind-man's buff.

101

THE WAGGON A-STOODED
Dree o'm a-ta'ken o't

(1) Well, here we be, then, wi' the vu'st poor lwoad
    O' vuzz we brought, a-stooded in the road.

(2) The road, George, no. There's na'r a road.
        That's wrong.
    If we'd a road, we mid ha' got along.

(1) Noo road ! Ees 'tis, the road that we do goo.

(2) Do goo, George, no. The pleace we can't get
        drough.

(1) Well, there, the vu'st lwoad we 've a-haul'd to
        day
    Is here a-stooded in thease bed o' clay.
    Here's rotten groun'! an' how the wheels do cut!
    The little woone's a-zunk up to the nut.

(3) An' yeet this rotten groun' don't reach a lug.

(1) Well, come, then, gi'e the plow another tug.

(2) They meares wull never pull the waggon out,
    A-lwoaded, an' a-stooded in thik rout.

(3) We'll try. Come, *Smiler*, come ! C'up, *White-
        voot*, gee !

(2) White-voot wi' lags all over mud ! Hee ! Hee !

(3) 'Twoon't wag. We shall but snap our gear,
    An' overstrain the meares. 'Twoon't wag,
        'tis clear.

(1) That's your work, William. No, in coo'se,
        'twoon't wag.
    Why did ye dreve en into thease here quag ?
    The vore-wheels be a-zunk above the nuts.

(3)   What then ?   I coulden leave the beaten track,
        To turn the waggon over on the back
        Ov woone o' theasem wheel-high emmet-butts.
        If you be sich a drever, an' do know't,
        You dreve the plow, then ; but you'll over-
            drow 't.
(1)   I dreve the plow, indeed ! Oh ! ees, what, now
        The wheels woont wag, then, *I* mid dreve the
            plow !
        We'd better dig away the groun' below
        The wheels. (2) There's na'r a speade to dig wi'.
(1)   An' teake an' cut a lock o' frith, an' drow
        Upon the clay. (2) Nor hook to cut a twig wi'.
(1)   Oh ! here's a bwoy a-comen. Here, my lad.
        Dost know vor a'r a speade, that can be had ?
(B)   At father's (1) Well, where's that ? (Bwoy)
           At Sam'el Riddick's.
(1)   Well run, an' ax vor woone. Fling up your
           heels,
        An' mind : a speade to dig out theasem wheels,
        An' hook to cut a little lock o' widdicks.
(3)   Why, we shall want zix ho'ses, or a dozen,
        To pull the waggon out, wi' all thease vuzzen.
(1)   Well, we mus' lighten en ; come, Jeames, then,
           hop
        Upon the lwoad, an' jus. fling off the top.
(2)   If I can clim' en ; but 'tis my consait,
        That I shall overzet en wi' my waight.
(1)   You overzet en ! No, Jeames, he won't vall,
        The lwoads' a-built so firm as any wall.
(2)   Here ! lend a hand or shoulder vor my knee
        Or voot. I'll scramble to the top an' zee
        What I can do. Well, here I be, among
        The fakkets, vor a bit, but not vor long.
        Heigh, George ! Ha ! ha ! Why this wull
           never stand.

(1)   Lo'k there, thik fellor is a-vell lik' lead,
       An' half the fuzzen wi 'n, heels over head !
       There's all the vuzz a-lyen lik' a staddle,
       An' he a-deab'd wi' mud. Oh ! Here's a caddle !

(3)   An' zoo you soon got down zome vuzzen,
              Jimmy.

(2)   Ees, I do know 'tis down, I brought it wi' me.

(3)   Your lwoad, George, wer a rather slick-built
              thing,
       But there, 'twer prickly vor the hands ! Did
              sting ?

(1)   Oh ! ees, d'ye teake me vor a nincompoop,
       No, no. The lwoad wer up so firm 's a rock,
       But two o' theasem emmet-butts would knock
       The tightest barrel nearly out o' hoop.

(3)   Oh ! now then, here's the bwoy a-bringen back
       The speade. Well done, my man. That
              idder slack.

(2)   Well done, my lad, sha't have a ho'se to ride
       When thou'st a meare. (Bwoy) Next never's-
              tide

(3)   Now let's dig out a spit or two
       O' clay, a-vore the little wheels ;
       Oh ! so's, I can't pull up my heels,
       I be a-stogg'd up over shoe.

(1)   Come, William, dig away! Why you do spuddle
       A'most so weak's a child. How you do muddle !
       Gi'e me the speade a-bit. A pig would rout
       It out a'most so nimbly wi' his snout.

(3)   Oh ! so's, d'ye hear it, then. How we can
              thunder !
       How big we be, then George ! what next I
              wonder ?

104

(1) Now, William, gi'e the waggon woone mwore
        twitch,
   The wheels be free, an' 'tis a lighter nitch.
(3) Come, *Smiler*, gee ! C'up *White-voot*. (1) That
        wull do.
(2) Do wag. (1) Do goo at last. (3) Well done.
        'Tis drough.
(1) Now, William, till you have mwore ho'ses' lags,
   Don't dreve the waggon into theasem quags.
(3) You build your lwoads up tight enough to ride.
(1) I can't do less, d'ye know, wi' you vor guide.

THE WIFE A-LOST

Since I noo mwore do zee your feace,
   Up steairs or down below,
I'll zit me in the lwonesome pleace
   Where flat-bough'd beech do grow :
Below the beeches' bough, my love,
   Where you did never come,
An' I don't look to meet ye now,
   As I do look at hwome.

Since you noo mwore be at my zide,
   In walks in zummer het,
I'll goo alwone where mist do ride,
   Drough trees a-drippen wet :
Below the rain-wet bough, my love,
   Where you did never come,
An' I don't grieve to miss ye now,
   As I do grieve at hwome.

Since now bezide my dinner-bwoard
   Your vaice do never sound,
I'll eat the bit I can avword
   A-vield upon the ground ;
Below the darksome bough, my love,
   Where you did never dine,
An' I don't grieve to miss ye now,
   As I at hwome do pine.

Since I do miss your vaice an' feace
   In prayer at eventide,
I'll pray wi' woone sad vaice vor greace
   To goo where you do bide ;
Above the tree an' bough, my love,
   Where you be gone avore,
An' be a waiten vor me now,
   To come vor evermwore.

READEN OV A HEAD-STWONE

As I wer readen ov a stwone
In Grenley church-yard all alwone,
A little maid ran up, wi' pride
To zee me there, an' push'd a-zide
A bunch o' bennets that did hide
   A verse her father, as she zaid,
   Put up above her mother's head,
      To tell how much he loved her :

The verse wer short, but very good,
I stood an' larn'd en where I stood :—
" Mid God, dear Meary, gi'e me greace
To vind, lik' thee, a better pleace,
Where I woonce mwore mid zee thy feace ;
   An' bring thy childern up to know
   His word, that they mid come an' show
      Thy soul how much I lov'd thee."

" Where's father, then," I zaid, "my chile?"
" Dead too," she answer'd wi' a smile ;
"An' I an' brother Jim do bide
At Betty White's, o' tother zide
O' road." "Mid He, my chile," I cried,
   " That's father to the fatherless,
   Become thy father now, an' bless,
      An' keep, an' lead, an' love thee,"

Though she've a-lost, I thought, so much,
Still He don't let the thoughts o't touch
Her litsome heart by day or night ;
An' zoo, if we could teake it right,
Do show He'll meake his burdens light
  To weaker souls, an' that his smile
  Is sweet upon a harmless chile,
    When they be dead that lov'd it.

THE MOTHER'S DREAM

I'd a dream to-night
As I fell asleep,
Oh ! the touching sight
Makes me still to weep :
Of my little lad,
Gone to leave me sad,
Aye, the child I had,
But was not to keep.

As in heaven high,
I my child did seek,
There, in train, came by
Children fair and meek,
Each in lily white,
With a lamp alight ;
Each was clear to sight,
But they did not speak.

Then, a little sad
Came my child in turn,
But the lamp he had,
Oh ! it did not burn ;
He, to clear my doubt,
Said, half turned about,
' Your tears put it out ;
Mother, never mourn.'

CHILDERN'S CHILDERN

Oh ! if my ling'ren life should run
   Drough years a-reckon'd ten by ten,
Below the never-tiren zun,
   Till beabes agean be wives an' men ;
An' stillest deafness should ha' bound
My ears at last vrom ev'ry sound ;
Though still my eyes in that sweet light
Should have the zight o' sky an' ground :
     Would then my steate
     In time so leate
Be jay or pain, be pain or jay ?

When Zunday then, a-weanen dim
   As thease that now's a-clwosen still,
Mid lose the zun's down-zinken rim
   In light behind the vire-bound hill ;
An' when the bells' last peal's a-rung,
An' I mid zee the wold an' young
A-vlocken by, but shoulden hear,
However near, a voot or tongue :
     Mid zuch a zight
     In that soft light
Be jay or pain, be pain or jay ?

If I should zee among em all,
   In merry youth a-gliden by,

My son's bwold son, a-grown man-tall,
  Or daughter's daughter, woman-high ;
An' she mid smile wi' your good feace,
  Or she mid walk your comely peäce,
But seem, although a-chatten loud,
So still's a cloud, in that bright pleace :
    Would youth so feair
    A-passen there
Be jay or pain, be pain or jay ?

Reading and
kneeling desk
for the family
prayers at Cam

Courtesy of Dorset
County Museum

WOAK HILL

When sycamore leaves wer a-spreaden
      Green-ruddy in hedges,
Bezide the red doust o' the ridges,
      A-dried at Woak Hill ;

I pack'd up my goods, all a-sheenen
      Wi' long years o' handlen
On dousty red wheels ov a waggon,
      To ride at Woak Hill.

The brown thatchen rwof o' the dwellen
      I then wer a-leaven,
Had shelter'd the sleek head o' Meary,
      My bride at Woak Hill.

But now vor zome years, her light voot-vall
      'S a-lost vrom the vlooren.
Too soon vor my jay an' my childern
      She died at Woak Hill .

But still I do think that, in soul,
      She do hover about us ;
To ho vor her motherless childern,
      Her pride at Woak Hill.

Zoo—lest she should tell me herea'ter
      I stole off 'ithout her,
An' left her, uncall'd at house-ridden,
      To bide at Woak Hill—

I call'd her so fondly, wi' lippens
    All soundless to others,
An' took her wi' air-reachen hand
    To my zide at Woak Hill.

On the road I did look round, a-talken
    To light at my shoulder,
An' then led her in at the doorway,
    Miles wide vrom Woak Hill.

An' that's why vo'k thought, vor a season,
    My mind wer a-wandren
Wi' sorrow, when I wer so sorely
    A-tried at Woak Hill.

But no ; that my Meary mid never
    Behold herzelf slighted,
I wanted to think that I guided
    My guide vrom Woak Hill.

THE GEATE A-VALLEN TO

(William Barnes's last dialect poem, dictated shortly before his death.)

In the sunsheen of our summers
    Wi' the haytime now a-come,
How busy wer we out a-vield
    Wi' vew a-left at hwome,
When waggons rumbled out ov yard
    Red wheeled, wi' body blue,
And back behind 'em loudly slamm'd
    The geate a'vallen to.

Drough day sheen for how many years
    The geate ha' now a-swung,
Behind the veet o' vull-grown men
    And vootsteps of the young
Drough years o' days it swung to us
    Behind each little shoe,
As we tripped lightly on avore
    The geate a-vallen to.

In evenen time o' starry night
    How mother zot at hwome
And kept her blazing vier bright
    Till father should ha' come,
And how she quickened up and smiled,

115

And stirred her vier anew,
To hear the trampen hosses' steps
And geate a-vallen to.

There's moonsheen now in nights o' Fall
When leaves be brown vrom green,
When to the slammen of the geate
Our Jenney's ears be keen,
When the wold dog do wag his tail,
And Jean could tell to who,
As he do come in drough the geate
The geate a-vallen to.

And oft do come a saddened hour
When there must goo away
One well-beloved to our heart's core,
Vor long, perhaps vor aye,
And oh ! it is a touchen thing
The loven heart must rue
To hear behind his last farewell
The geate a-vallen to.

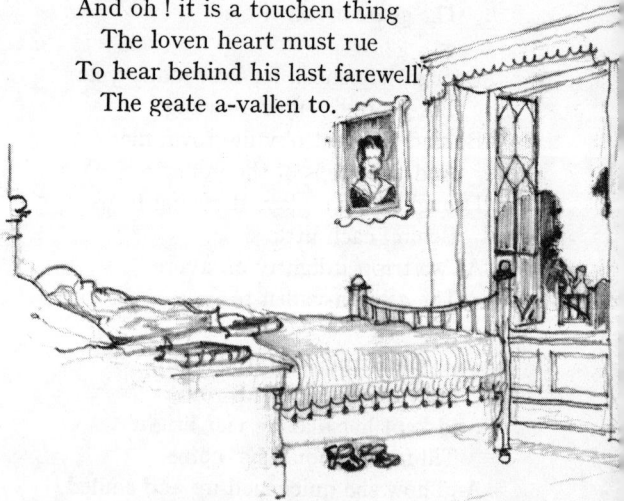

"An when our hands to vall
to rest, It mid be vrom
a work a-blest"

Whitcombe

Came

The resting place

After Word
Poems Grave and Gay

Giles Dugdale's *Poems Grave and Gay*, first pub-
lished in 1949, selected only sixty from the eight
hundred or so poems written by Barnes. Dugdale
chose fifty dialect poems and only ten in standard
English. This judgement conflicts with that of the
editor of *Macmillan's Magazine* in 1864, who wrote
to the poet to persuade him to prefer common
English for his poetry and thus to attain a wider
readership. 'What a pity Mr. Barnes *will* write that
dialect.', one reader complained, 'I really cannot,
even after much pains, get at the meaning, and the
effort too often exhausts the interest.' In the event it
is Dugdale's judgement which most probably concurs
with that of the common reader. Barnes is most
widely remembered and appreciated as a dialect poet.

Barnes fully recognised the disadvantages of
writing in dialect. Writing in a fast-wearing out
speech form, he said, was 'as idle as the writing one's
name in the snow of a spring day'. Yet he testified
that the Dorset was for him 'the only true speech of
the life that I draw'. This is not to say that he began
his career as a poet by writing in dialect; his first two
books of poetry were in common English. In addition,
he acceded to Macmillan's request in 1868 by publish-
ing his *Poems of Rural life in common English*, yet
this event did not perceptibly alter the general
preference for his dialect poems.

How may we explain this preference? Part of the answer may be obtained by comparing two of his poems on the same theme, that of the lost wife. 'Plorata Veris Lachrymis' is in common English while 'The Wife A-Lost' is in the Dorset. The English poem has undoubted pathos, especially in the repetitive hopelessness of the fourth verse. Nevertheless, one feels that the speaking voice in the poem is not a distinctive one. The sentiments and language could be that of any number of verse craftsmen of the eighteenth or nineteenth centuries. Its diction is conventional and predictable: hope/zest, east/west, woe, grief, weal, boon. The metaphor is commonplace; death 'unlocks' the hands of the lovers.

By contrast, the Dorset poem establishes, from the outset, the sound of a particular voice; homely, subdued, grief-stricken. The imagery is more concrete and particularised; the speaker notices, almost without noticing, the flat beech boughs and the dripping branches. Though less melodramatic than a traditional ballad, the poem takes on the cadences of such pieces as 'The Unquiet Grave' and the mood is almost as austere. The desolate widower in 'The Wife A-Lost' quits his home as much as possible to avoid painful associations:

> 'I'll eat the bit I can avword
> A-vield upon the ground;'

The shared communion of the family supper has given way to the solitary eating of a 'bit'. There are suggestions here of a (newly-acquired?) poverty and also of a lack of care for his own welfare by the speaker. He prefers to sit upon the ground in what is both symbolically and actually a dark and wet season. Yet the words are from the dialect; in Wessex people do talk of eating a 'bit o' bread'.

The dialect poems are generally more concrete, vivid, and dramatically realised than those in common English. Dialect words, because they are more specific in association, communicate a more particular, and therefore sharper, picture of life. Merely to read through Barnes's *Glossary of the Dorset Dialect* is to be put in touch not only with the roots of our language but also of our society. The terminology is rich with associations and traditions from a bygone rural life. In choosing the dialect, Barnes also chose a narrower but richer range of associations than those available in standard English. His choice was intuitively correct. Despite the achievement of some of the English poems such as 'Rustic Childhood' and 'White and Blue', it is in the dialect that his voice is most distinctive and his sensibility most effectively communicated. Gerard Manley Hopkins considered Barnes's use of dialect 'a sort of unfair play'. It *is* unfair in that it was not available to all poets. Hopkins believed that the advantage of dialect is that it 'sort of guarantees the spontaneousness of the consciousness of the thought'. In his own work, Hopkins had no such advantage and was forced to invent his own language to 'guarantee' the spontaneity and truth of his poems. Each of these poets found it necessary to turn away from the thinness of nineteenth century English to other more vital sources.

Barnes's work is often compared with that of Clare and Burns. He has not the profound intensity of the best work of the former nor the passion and lyricism of the latter but, because of the richness of his

Dorsetshire idiom, his county is realised more vividly than the Northamptonshire of Clare or the Ayrshire of Burns. It is more fruitful to consider his work in connection with that of two other poets, Hopkins and Hardy. Hopkins declared himself a 'great admirer' of Barnes. He was fascinated with Barnes's technical achievements as well as the content of the poems. These two poets shared an interest in philology and stylistics; each of them experimented with verse techniques found in Anglo-Saxon and Welsh poetry. Natural beauty is a common theme for them though their attitudes to it are very different. Hopkins's attitude is primarily aesthetic. In 'Binsey Poplars' the felling of the trees inspires in him a passionate and delicate grief for fallen beauty. Barnes looks at nature through the eye of the countryman. The speaker in 'Vellen the Tree' recalls fond memories with which the rural labourers associate the 'girt elem tree'; he personifies the tree with its 'wold head' and swaying limbs; yet, when it comes to it, he enjoys the bit of fun in cutting it down and accepts philosophically that the 'girt elem tree' that was standing this morning is now 'a-cut down'.

Hopkins was, of course, pre-eminently, a religious poet. Barnes, like Hopkins, was in orders, and was dubbed by Llewelyn Powys 'the last of the believers'. He was most certainly a pious scholar and a cleric, a Christian and a poet, but he was never a 'Christian poet'. That is to say that his poetry never attempts the impassioned re-enactment of Christian experience which is characteristic of Hopkins's verse. Barnes is a religious poet only in the sense that his writing is replete with a sense of the holiness of all things.

In his poem 'The Last Signal', Hardy described how the sunlight reflected to him from Barnes's coffin seemed like a last wave of the hand from his old friend. He had much reason for gratitude to Barnes. Implicit in Barnes's verse are some of the major themes of Hardy's later novels and poems. One of these is the sense of the passing away of the old rural life and its replacement by the new, mass-produced civilisation of Victorian England. It is a theme to be seen in Hardy's earliest work; in the novel 'Under the Greenwood Tree' (1872), for example, he recounts how the village choir is to be replaced by the newly-fashionable church organ. In his first dialect collection Barnes had included 'The Settle An' The Girt Wood Fire' which had contrasted, with sadness and humour, the great open fire of yore with the 'little hole to teake a little grate o' coal', and the comfortable old settle with the new chairs and couches covered with anti-macassars and still too fine to be comfortable. As a nature poet, Hardy learned much from Barnes, as is shown by a comparison of Hardy's 'Weathers' with 'Tokens' in the present volume. Finally, the theme of the dead wife, so splendidly explored by Hardy in such poems as 'The Voice', is to be found here in 'The Wife A-Lost' and the profoundly-moving 'Woak Hill'. Hardy must have known of, and learned from, these poems.

When the diarist, Francis Kilvert, visited the aged Barnes on the last day of April 1874, the poet spoke of Tennyson's 'Northern Farmer' which was, he believed, marred by the poet's lack of sympathy for his subject. Barnes then declared that 'in all which he himself had written there was not a line which was not inspired by love for & kindly sympathy with the things and people described'. Lucy Baxter reports her father as saying: 'There is no art without love. Every artist who has produced anything worthy has had a love of his subject.' In this statement Barnes signifies that he understands the primary impulse of his own work which is animated throughout by a profound sympathy with his subject matter. His work may lack the passion, intensity and variety to be found in other poets but this lack is more than recompensed by the loving serenity that pervades his pages.

Barnes is, above all, a celebratory poet who affirms the value and beauty of even the most commonplace of human experiences. It is interesting to note just how frequently the word 'love' appears on his pages:

'I knew you young, and love you now,
O shining grass, and shady bough.'
        and
'But still, sweet spot, wherever I may be,
My love-led soul will wander back to thee.'
        and
'Vor I do love noo tree so well
'S the girt woak tree that's in the dell.'

He cannot bear the denial of love as exemplified in the rejection of 'The Love Child':

'Oh! it meade me a'most teary-ey'd,
An' I vound I a'most could ha' groan'd – –
What! so winnen, an' still cast a-zide – –
What! so lovely, an' not to be own'd;'

The pages of *Poems Grave and Gay* are crowded with sentiments of affection for the trees, leaves, flowers, people and places that he knows. Most of all he loves people, such as 'Aunt', even when in one of her 'tantrums'. Dugdale includes here two beautiful and humorous character portraits: that of 'The Shy Man', whose simple goodness of heart outweighs the absurdity of his timorous conduct; and that of 'Gammony Gay', whose infectious good nature communicates itself even to the animals and birds. Perhaps Barnes's finest expression in this mode is the dramatic monologue 'Vull A Man', an astonishingly vigorous and forthright declaration of mature malehood.

The world depicted in these poems is that of the eighteenth-century rural life into which Barnes was born in Blackmoor Vale. His themes are those of the beauties of nature, the quality and variety of men and women, homely incidents, jokes (see 'What Dick An' I Did'), reminiscences of childhood, rural dialogues or 'eclogues', domestic joys, fatherhood, marriage, the family, descendants, the hearth and the table. He enjoys the age-long rivalry between town and country and is always on the side of the latter. 'Sam'el Down Vrom Lon'on' tells of the boastful townee come into the country; 'John Bloom In Lon'on' tells of the visit paid by the gigantic miller to the Crystal Palace Exhibition and his inability to enter a cab because the door is too small. Despite this fact, he complains to the driver that he is a Dorset man 'shrunk so thin to bwone an' skin', presumably because of the inadequate London diet.

The tone of these poems varies from nostalgia to humour and the sly comedy of the eclogues. The two exceptions here are to be found in 'A Witch' and 'False Friends-Like'. The former is a spirited dramatic monologue about the 'wold hag', Moll Brown, and the blight she throws upon things. The vindictive note of the conclusion may appal the modern reader but would have seemed a natural reaction in the rural society in which the poet was born. In fact, cruelty both sickened and embarrassed Barnes. The 'false friend' of his childhood was a bigger boy who promised him a ride in a wheelbarrow, then tipped him out. Now, he confesses, when a man comes to him 'so thick-like' he is suspicious and feels a little shy.

Such poems are exceptional. Almost all his themes inspire affection in him, even for the name of a village now almost entirely passed away. The bachelor's lonely life provokes his sympathy; he appreciates the energy and merriment of the farmer's sons; he delights in the fiddler who spreads joy round him at the 'randy'; he loves to share the innocent conceit of the young man showing off his flashy new clothes to two giggling girls. Most of all, his heart is touched by the tokens of scenes from his childhood, such as the shoes left by 'Grammer', which bring the old lady back to mind. His loving imagination irradiates these simple scenes so that they are made bright for his readers. If the key-word to his life is 'industry', that to his poems is 'love'.

Alan Chedzoy

South Street, Dorchester in the 19th century . . .

William Barnes set up a school in Durngate Street, moving later to Norman's House just north of Napier's Almshouses. A further move was made to No 40 South Street on the west side of South Street right opposite the ancient (and rival) Hardye's School.

GLOSSARY

(A guide to Dorset words and expressions found in the context of poems in this text)

A-cothed: diseased
A-dreven: driven
A-stogged: having one's feet stuck in dirt or clay
A-stooded: sunk into the ground
A-strout: stretched out stiffly
Athirt: athwart, across
Axed: asked
Beane: bane, poison
Be'mi'ster: Beaminster
Bennets: the stems and heads of flowers
Bist: beest, is
Blather: a bladder
Bron; bran, orbackbron, backbran: a brand, a big log of wood at the back of the fire
Bwoth: both
Caddle: a muddle
Childern: children
Clavy: a mantel-piece
Clomb: climbed
Clote: the yellow water-lily (nuphar lutea)
Coll: to take one fondly round the neck
Consait: conceit, fancy
Crope: crept
Crowd: a fiddle
Culver: a wood pigeon or ring dove

Dawk: push
Droat: throat
Drongway: a narrow way between two hedges or walls
Drow: to throw
Eegrass:
Ees: yes
Eet: yet
Elem: elm
Eltrot: eltroot, the cow parsley
Emmet-but: an ant-hill
Fakket: faggot, a bundle of sticks
Fay: to fit, to succeed
Feace: face
For aye: for ever
Frith: brushwood
Gil'cup: the buttercup
Girt: great, big
Goocoo: the cuckoo
Graegle: the wild hyacinth
Handy: near
Hag-rod: hag-ridden
Hangen: the sloping side of a hill
Hauk: cough
He'th: the hearth
Het: heat, also to hit
Ho: care
Hodmadod: a dump or mess
Holler: hollow, vale
Housen: houses
Hwomely: homely
In coose: of course
Jay: joy
Jowl: party, merrymaking (poss. from joviality)

Lew: lee, shelter from the wind
Limber: limp
Lug: a pole, 5½ yards
Meare: a mare
Me'th: mirth
Min: mind, mind you
Moot: stump
Muddy-lagged: legs covered with mud
Mwoldren: mouldering
Narn: never a one, not one
Nitch: a burden, a load
Noggerhead: a loggerhead, a blockhead
Nut: the stock of a wheel
Nwone: no one
Orts: leavings from the hay with which cows are fed
in the field
Pank: to pant
Perty: pretty
Piny: peony
Pitch: to put up hay
Plim: to swell out
Ply: to bend
Poll: head
Pook: large cones of drying hay
Popple: pebble
Pummy: apple-pummace from the cider wring
Randy: a party
Readship: counsel
Reely: to dance reels
Rout: a rut
Rudge: ridge of roof
Ruf: roof
Rue: sorrow

Scram: screwy, dwarfish
Sheaded: shaded
Shere: shire, county
Shouds: shrouds, the heads of trees
Skimmy: to mow the bunches of rank grass in a summerleaze
Snabble: to snap up hastily or greedily
Snead: the pole of a scythe
Soulzight: the inner vision
Span-new: brand-new
Spitish: spiteful, snappish
Sprack: lively, active
Spweil: spoil
Spuddle: to dig slightly and incontinuously
Squilched: squeezed
Squot: to flatten as by a blow
Staddle: a wooden frame to support a rick
Tay: a toy
Teazen: teasing
Tedding: the throwing abroad of mown grass so that it may dry
There's n'ar a road: there is never (not) a road
This idden: this isn't
Tillage: digging
Towse: a slight blow with the hand
Trig: to prop up or hold up
Tun: the chimney-top up from the ridge of the house
Tutty: a bunch of flowers or nosegay
Twite: to reproach or twit
Veag: wrath, anger
Vearies: fairies
Vind: find
Vinny: blue vinny cheese

Vo'k: folk, people
Vooten: footing
Vooty: unhandily small
Vuzz: furze
Wag: to stir or go
Wallen: walls
Werden: were not
Widdick: a small withy or rod
Whindlen: small and weakly
Wink: winch or crank
Woone: one
Whurr: to fling overarm
Zoo: so
Zot: sat
Zull: a plough

St. Peters Church, the Dorset
County Museum & the William
Barnes Statue, Dorchester

us hear the conclusion of all tho God & keep his Commandments, for that toucheth all men for God

Interior. Winterborne
Came Church.